JN131786

News Reports from Japan's Next Generation

Future Times

Paul Stapleton   **Atsuko Uemura**

NATIONAL
GEOGRAPHIC
LEARNING

Australia · Brazil · Mexico · Singapore · United Kingdom · United States

Future Times—News Reports from Japan's Next Generation

Paul Stapleton / Atsuko Uemura

© 2020 Cengage Learning K.K.

Photo Credits:
Cover: © Krzysztof Baranowski/Moment/Getty Images
p. 10: © Jiji Press Photo; p. 16: © AFP=Jiji; p. 22: © Jiji Press Photo;
p. 28: © LauriPatterson/iStock.com; p. 34: © Archives21/Pacific Press Service;
p. 40: © Alamy/Pacific Press Service; p. 46 © The Asahi Shimbun/Jiji Press Photo;
p. 52: © TAGSTOCK1/iStock.com; p. 58 © Science Source/Pacific Press Service;
p. 64: © Juanmonino/iStock.com; p. 70: © AFP=Jiji; p. 76: © recep-bg/iStock.com;
p. 82: © Alamy/Pacific Press Service; p. 88: © EPA=Jiji; p. 94: © pius99/iStock.com

For permission to use material from this textbook or product, e-mail to **eltjapan@cengage.com**

ISBN: 978-4-86312-367-0

National Geographic Learning | Cengage Learning K.K.
No. 2 Funato Building 5th Floor
1-11-11 Kudankita, Chiyoda-ku
Tokyo 102-0073
Japan

Tel: 03-3511-4392
Fax: 03-3511-4391

Preface

Predicting the future is said to be a fool's game. Fifty years ago, many people thought that we would have colonies on the moon by now. On the other hand, just 30 years ago, we could not have imagined that mobile phones would perform so many functions.

In some senses, the future has already arrived. Artificial intelligence (AI) has become part of our lives. Robots are starting to take care of our elderly. Social media constantly gives us suggestions about what to buy, often as if it already knows our tastes in books, music, etc. However, this is just the beginning. But not all changes come from new technology. Society is also changing. For example, the way we feel about foreigners and immigration in Japan is shifting as the world becomes more globalized. And then there is the huge issue of climate change and how we will adapt to a warmer world and rising sea levels.

In *Future Times*, we make 15 bold predictions about Japan's future by starting each chapter with a fictionalized news story. Then, we analyze the possibilities based on recent trends. Each chapter has exercises for learners to critically think about the topics and express their opinions.

Paul Stapleton

まえがき

皆さんの目に今の日本はどのように映っていますか。またこれからの日本はどのようであればいいと思いますか。本書の各課は数十年後の日本を想定し、そこで起こる架空のニュース記事から始まります。これから数十年後の日本、それはまさに皆さんが築いていく日本です。数十年後はSF映画に登場する夢のような想像の世界ではありません。現状の分析と考察により、予測可能な未来です。英語を学習しながら、日本の未来を予測してみませんか。

課のトピックは「雇用」「日本文化」「気候変動」「交通輸送」など多岐にわたります。それぞれのトピックについて語彙学習、リーディング、リスニング、ライティングなど様々な活動を行いながら、日本の現状の把握、そして分析を行い、架空のNewsが現実になる可能性を考えます。そして皆さん一人一人が分析家となって巻末のReportを作成してください。

インターネットが世界をつないだ今、どの国も他の国々との関係性を考えずに進むことはできないでしょう。英語で日本の現状とこれからを学習することが、未来を築いていく皆さんの役に立つことを願っています。

上村淳子

■Contents

本書の構成と使い方

本書は全 15 課（News 1 ～ 15）で構成されています。巻末には、各 News の Report を収録しています。

各 News の構成と使い方

各 News は、巻末の Report を含め計 8 ページ構成です。セクションやアクティビティの基本的な内容や使い方は次のとおりです。

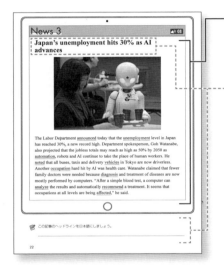

News

数十年後の日本を想定して書かれた架空のニュース記事です。

ヘッドライン

　ニュース記事のヘッドライン、つまり見出しを日本語で考えます。ヘッドラインは、記事の内容を最も端的にまとめた、いわば記事のエッセンスです。記事に英語で付けられているヘッドラインは、日本語の新聞ならどんな見出しになるかを考えましょう。

　英語のヘッドラインでは、過去は現在形で、未来は現在分詞で、進行形や受動態は be 動詞を省略、冠詞の省略など、限られたスペースで語数を減らすための工夫がされていることが多いので注意しましょう。

Vocabulary Check

　まず記事にざっと目を通し、提示されている日本語の意味を持つ単語や語句を下線部から探しましょう。日本語から英語を探すのではなく、文脈から下線の単語や語句の意味を考え、その適切な日本語訳を提示の中から選ぶようにすると、リーディング力の向上に効果があります。

Comprehension

　Vocabulary Check で語彙を確認した後、もう一度記事を通して読み、日本語で要旨を完成させましょう。

Report Completion

　巻末の Report に取り組みましょう。

Report（巻末に掲載）

I 記者が要点を取材メモに記入するように、空所を埋めて各記事の内容を整理しましょう。

II 記事に書かれている出来事が未来の日本で起きる可能性を考え、その自分の予想をパーセンテージで表します。記事を読んだ後の印象で決めてください。この段階では、まだ詳しく分析する必要はありません。

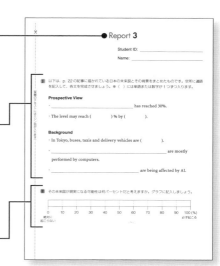

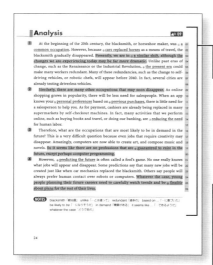

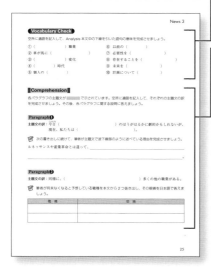

Analysis

先に読んだニュース記事に書かれている未来の出来事が将来、実際に起こるかどうかを日本や世界の現状から考察したエッセイ調の文章です。

Vocabulary Check

Analysis にある下線部の単語や語句の日本語の意味を考えます。辞書を使わず、文脈から考えましょう。その後、辞書で答えを確認したり、授業で他の受講生と確認し合ったりするとよいでしょう。

Comprehension

Analysis の内容をパラグラフごとに理解していきます。News 1 〜 7 では、各パラグラフの主題文（トピックセンテンス）を で提示してあります。主題文とは、パラグラフの中で最も端的にそのトピックを紹介する文です。通常 1 つのパラグラフは 1 つのトピックでまとまっています。

News 8 〜 15 では、自分で各パラグラフの主題文を探して書き出しましょう。

主題文以外の文は、解説したり例を挙げたりして、そのトピックの理解を助ける働きをしています。トピックを明確に理解した上でパラグラフを読み、設問に答えましょう。

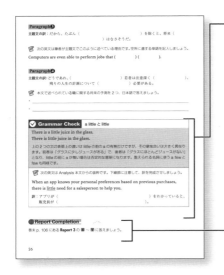

Grammar Check

　Analysis で使われている文法事項を 1 つ取り上げ、簡潔に説明しています。その内容を確認した後、実際にその文法事項が使われている本文中の英文を日本語に訳してみましょう。

　英文を読むには、その構造を理解する必要があります。文法を理解することは英文の構造を理解することなので、文法確認はリーディング力を伸ばすのにとても大切な学習です。

Report Completion

巻末の Report に取り組みましょう。

Report（巻末に掲載）

Ⅲ　Analysis の内容に関して 5 つの意見が提示されています。その意見に賛成か反対かを答え、課のトピックに対する自分の考えを整理しましょう。

Ⅳ　再度、冒頭の記事の出来事が未来の日本で起きる可能性を考え、パーセンテージで表します。ここでは Analysis で読んだ分析をもとにして、その可能性について考えてください。Ⅱで答えた数値から変化はあるでしょうか。

Ⅴ　記事と Analysis で論じられている日本の未来について、自分がどのように考えるのかを言葉にしてみましょう。英語と日本語のどちらで書くかは担当教員の指示に従ってください。

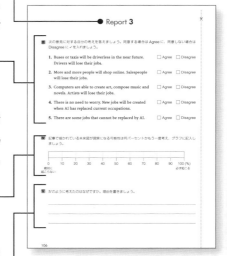

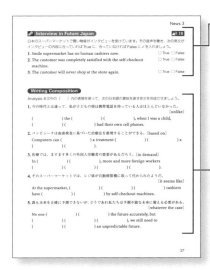

Interview in Future Japan

リスニング問題です。2人の会話を聴き、提示の英文がその内容と合っているかどうかを答えます。

会話の内容はニュース記事と Analysis で述べられている事柄に関連しており、記事の出来事が起きている未来の日本で、アメリカ人の記者がインタビューしているという設定です。

Writing Composition

記事や Analysis で使われている、覚えておくと役立つ表現を5つ取り上げました。提示されている表現を使って日本語の意味に合う英文を完成させましょう。余裕があれば、その表現を用いて自分で自由に英文を作ってみましょう。

音声ファイルの利用方法

https://ngljapan.com/ft-audio

🔊 00 のアイコンがある箇所の音声ファイルにアクセスできます。

❶ 上記の URL にアクセス、または右の QR コードをスマートフォンなどのリーダーでスキャン

❷ 希望の番号をクリックして音声ファイルを再生またはダウンロード

無料のオンライン学習ツール Quizlet でボキャビル！

https://quizlet.com/NGL_Japan/folders/future-times/sets

上記の URL にアクセス、または右の QR コードをスマートフォンなどのリーダーでスキャンすると、News 1〜15 の1つ目の **Vocabulary Check** で取り上げている語句をクイズ形式で手軽に学習することができます。

Cash loses out to electronic money

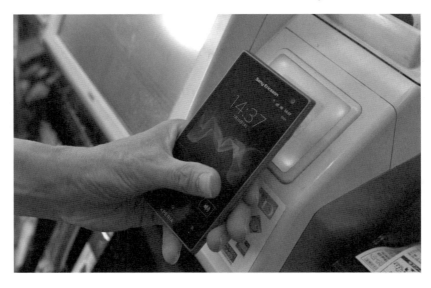

The Ministry of Finance announced today that it will no longer be producing any paper notes or coins as of next month. Along with the announcement came the declaration that all forms of cash, both notes and coins, will no longer be legal tender as of January 1, 2041. From that date forward, all types of purchases will be performed electronically. The Ministry advises the public to take their cash to banks before December 31 to have it credited to their accounts. After that date, all cash will become worthless. Ministry spokesperson, Aoi Kurihara, urged the public to bring in their cash well before the end of the year to avoid long queues on December 31.

 この記事のヘッドラインを日本語にしましょう。

Vocabulary Check

次の意味に該当するものを記事中の下線を引いた単語または語句から抜き出しましょう。ただし、動詞は原形で答えましょう。

1. …を避ける _____
2. 公示 _____
3. 電子装置で _____
4. 列 _____
5. 紙幣 _____
6. 価値がない _____
7. 法定貨幣 _____
8. 口座 _____
9. （口座に）記入する _____
10. 購入 _____

Comprehension

空所に適語を記入して、記事の要旨を完成させましょう。

財務省は来月以降（   ）と発表した。それに伴い、2041 年 1 月 1 日以降（   ）が法定貨幣でなくなり、すべての購入は（   ）ことになるため、同省は（   ）までに現金を銀行口座に入れるよう国民に勧めている。

Report Completion

巻末 p. 101 にある **Report 1** の **I** と **II** に答えましょう。

Analysis

1   Money, in one form or another, has been with us since the ①beginning of agriculture, close to 10,000 years ago. ② In ancient times, trading domestic animals and food products led to a cash economy. About 5,000 years ago, ③metal objects were used to ④symbolize certain standard amounts of food, cattle, sheep or salt. Then, around 3,000 years ago, coins and paper money appeared, and they have been with us ever since.

2   Paper notes and coins have lasted an ⑤incredibly long time without much change; however, credit cards, and more recently, online payments are changing our concept of money very quickly. Although Japanese have been ⑥comparatively reluctant to use credit cards, the story may be quite different concerning e-commerce, which is the term used for payment via the Internet.

3   Presently, China is the world leader in e-commerce. In many senses, 2040 has already arrived there. The main reason is the instant messaging app, WeChat, which is the Chinese equivalent of LINE. The key, of course, has been the smartphone. Because almost everyone has one, it has become ⑦a substitute for cash. Simply place your phone over a scanner, and the payment is complete. Now in China, there are more than one billion WeChat users, many of whom pay for almost everything with their phones. They can even ⑧exchange gifts just by transferring electronic money to a ⑨recipient. Using one's phone to make payments in China is now so common that some businesses do not even want to receive cash.

4   In fact, many people in Japan are very attached to cash so it will probably disappear very slowly. However, the convenience of using an app on a mobile phone to make payments is very attractive. The young generation in Japan, which has grown up with smartphones, is likely to find e-commerce using their phones ⑩hard to resist. At some point in the future, surely we will have no need for a wallet.

01
02
03
04
05
06
07
08
09
10
11
12
13
14
15
16
17
18
19
20
21
22
23
24

NOTES   in one form or another「何らかの形で」 close to ...「…に近い」 domestic animals「家畜」
lead to ...「…につながる」 be reluctant to *do*「…するのは気が進まない」
concerning「…について」 via「…経由で」 equivalent「匹敵するもの」
transfer「…を送る」 so ～ that ...「とても～なので…」
be attached to ...「…に愛着がある」 be likely to *do*「…しそうだ」

Vocabulary Check

空所に適語を記入して、Analysis 本文中の下線を引いた単語や語句の意味を完成させましょう。

① （　　　　　　　）の始まり

② （　　　　　　　）においては

③ 金属の（　　　　　　）

④ （　　　　　　　）

⑤ （　　　　　　　　　　　）長い

⑥ （　　　　　　　　　　）

⑦ 現金の（　　　　　　　）

⑧ 贈り物を（　　　　　　　　）

⑨ （　　　　　　　）

⑩ （　　　　　　　）ことが困難で

Comprehension

各パラグラフの主題文が ▨▨▨▨▨ で示されています。空所に適語を記入して、それぞれの主題文の訳を完成させましょう。その後、各パラグラフに関する設問に答えましょう。

Paragraph❶

主題文の訳：お金は何らかの形で、（　　　　　　　　　　　　　　　　　　　　）からずっと
（　　　　　　　　　　　　　　　　　　）。

✎ 空所に適語を記入して、お金の歴史について整理しましょう。

約 1 万年前：（　　　　　　　）が始まり、お金も誕生

約 5000 年前：（　　　　　　　　　　　　　　　　　　）するのに（　　　　　　　　）を使用

約 3000 年前：（　　　　　　　　　　）が出現

Paragraph❷

主題文の訳：紙幣と硬貨は（　　　　　　　　　　　　　　　　　　）存続し
てきた。しかし、（　　　　　　　　　　　　　　　　　　　　）
が私たちのお金の概念を急速に変えつつある。

✎ 次の質問に英語で答えましょう。

Do many Japanese people prefer credit cards to cash?

― _____

Paragraph❸

主題文の訳：現在、中国は（　　　　　　　　　　　　　　　　　　　　　　　　　　　　）。

 次の英文は中国の電子商取引について述べたものです。本文の内容と合うように、空所に適する単語を記入しましょう。

1. (　　　　　　) is the messaging app used by more than one billion people in China.

2. Today, almost every Chinese has a (　　　　　　), and they use it to make payments.

3. Chinese can send and receive gifts using (　　　　　) (　　　　　) without any cash involved.

Paragraph❹

主題文の訳：将来いつか、（　　　　　　　　　　　　　　　　　　　　　　　　　　　）。

 これまでと今後の日本人の支払い方法に関する筆者の考えを、次の英語のキーワードすべてをヒントとして使って日本語でまとめましょう。

| a smartphone | attached | cash | convenience | the young generation |

_____

_____

✅ Grammar Check　使役を表す have

＜have ＋目的語＋動詞の原形／動詞の過去分詞＞で、「～に…してもらう」あるいは「～を…してもらう」といった使役の意味になります。動詞は、目的語（大半は「人」）がその行為をする場合には原形、目的語（大半は「物」）がその行為をされる（受ける）場合には過去分詞になります。次の２つの文を比較しましょう。

I **had** *him* repair the door.（彼にドアを修理してもらった）

I **had** *the door* repaired.（ドアを修理してもらった）

 次の英文は記事からの抜粋です。下線部に注意して、訳を完成させしましょう。

The Ministry advises the public to take their cash to banks before December 31 to <u>have it credited</u> to their accounts.

訳：財務省は国民に、（　　　　　　　　　　　　　　　　　　　）を持って行き、（　　　　　　　　　　　　）ことを勧めている。

● Report Completion

巻末 p. 102 にある **Report 1** の **Ⅲ** 〜 **Ⅴ** に答えましょう。

🖊 Interview in Future Japan　🔊 04

日本で買い物をしていた中国人旅行者がインタビューを受けています。その音声を聴き、次の英文がインタビューの内容に合っていれば True に、合っていなければ False に ✓ を入れましょう。

1. The Chinese tourist needed a lot of cash for shopping in Japan.　□ True □ False

2. The Chinese tourist came to Japan more than five times.　□ True □ False

3. The Chinese tourist thinks we need cash even in the world of e-commerce.　□ True □ False

Writing Composition

Analysis 本文中の [　] 内の表現を使って、次の日本語の意味を表す英文を完成させましょう。

1. スマートフォンの普及が買い物での電子商取引へとつながった。[lead to]

The spread of (　　　　　　) (　　　　　　) (　　　　　　)
(　　　　　　) in (　　　　　　).

2. 概して、古い世代は支払いにスマートフォンを使うことに気が進まない。
[be reluctant to *do*]
Generally, the older generation (　　　　　　) (　　　　　　)
(　　　　　　) (　　　　　　) their smartphone for (　　　　　　).

3. WeChat はとても便利なので、10 億人以上の中国人が利用している。[so 〜 that ...]
WeChat (　　　　　　) (　　　　　　) (　　　　　　) (　　　　　　)
(　　　　　　) (　　　　　　) one (　　　　　　) Chinese use it.

4. 私はこの財布を 10 年以上使っていて、愛着がある。[be attached to]
I (　　　　　　) (　　　　　　) (　　　　　　) this wallet (　　　　　　)
more than 10 years, so I (　　　　　　) really (　　　　　　) (　　　　　　) it.

5. 現金はいつか消滅しそうだと思いますか。[be likely to *do*]
Do you think that (　　　　　　) (　　　　　　) (　　　　　　)
(　　　　　　) (　　　　　　) some day?

Japanime overtakes Disneyland as world's most popular theme park

Japanime, the incredibly popular theme park that has spread rapidly around the world, is now more popular than Disneyland. Attendance figures show that Japanime's four parks combined received more visitors than Disneyland worldwide for the first time last year. Japanime opened its first park in 2030 in Fukuoka, followed by three more in Paris, San Francisco and Shanghai in the 2030s. This expansion is due to the explosive interest worldwide in Japanese culture, which includes anime, manga and food, such as sushi. A spokesperson for Japanime commented, "Of course, we are pleased about the growth in our attendance figures, but we are more concerned about the quality of the experience we provide to our guests. We really want our international visitors to feel the warmth of Japanese hospitality."

 この記事のヘッドラインを日本語にしましょう。

Vocabulary Check

次の意味に該当するものを記事中の下線を引いた単語または語句から抜き出しましょう。ただし、動詞は原形で答えましょう。

1. 入場者数　_____
2. おもてなし　_____
3. 拡大　_____
4. 広まる　_____
5. 成長　_____
6. …を合わせる　_____
7. …を含む　_____
8. 爆発的な　_____
9. …を提供する　_____
10. 気づかっていて　_____

Comprehension

空所に適語を記入して、記事の要旨を完成させましょう。

日本のテーマパーク「ジャパニメ」が4つのパークの入場者数を合計して、昨年（
　　　　　　）。福岡から始まり、パリ、サンフランシスコ、上海と拡大して
いるのは、（　　　　　　　　　　　　　　　　　　）によるものだ。広報担当者は、
ジャパニメは（　　　　　　　）よりも、（　　　　　　　　　　　　　）に心を配り、
（　　　　　　　　　　　　　）を感じてもらいたいと話している。

Report Completion

巻末 p. 103 にある **Report 2** の **I** と **II** に答えましょう。

Analysis

1　Although Japan is famous around the world for its high-quality products, until quite ₀₁
recently, Japan has had few ① cultural exports. However, in the past generation or so, ₀₂
there has been an explosion of interest in Japanese culture. Before the 1980s, outside of ₀₃
Japan, eating at a Japanese restaurant was considered ② an exotic experience, if you were ₀₄
lucky enough to find one. Now, in many parts of the world, the problem is not finding a ₀₅
Japanese restaurant, but rather, it is having to ③ wait in line to get in. Likewise, most ₀₆
supermarkets in Asian and Western countries have a sushi section. In many countries, ₀₇
people now associate the word "Hokkaido" with high quality food products. ₀₈

2　This ④ great increase in cultural exports from Japan is not confined to food. A ₀₉
generation ago, the words "manga," "anime" and "emoji" did not ⑤ exist in the English ₁₀
language. Now, not only have these words become commonly used in English, but their ₁₁
popularity has ⑥ advanced to the point where they have become part of mainstream ₁₂
culture. ₁₃

3　Interestingly, these Japanese cultural exports have been ⑦ absorbed into the local ₁₄
overseas cultures and ⑧ adapted to suit the local people's taste. The California sushi roll ₁₅
with its crab and avocado is available everywhere in North America, and is one of the ₁₆
earliest adaptations of Japanese culture. Although traditional Japanese may think the ₁₇
California roll is not real sushi, all cultures embrace ideas from abroad and then adapt ₁₈
them. Japanese curry is a good example of this. ₁₉

4　Japan's cultural exports have most recently ⑨ expanded beyond food and art forms, ₂₀
such as anime and manga, to the virtual and behavioral worlds. Virtual pets like ₂₁
Pokémon are on the smartphones of millions around the world. As for behavior, ₂₂
companies, such as Uniqlo and Muji, are teaching staff in their overseas branches how ₂₃
to treat customers in the Japanese way of hospitality. ₂₄

5　While it may be unlikely that a Japanese theme park ⑩ conquers the world, it seems ₂₅
like Japan's culture has already had a big international influence and will continue to ₂₆
grow in the future. ₂₇

NOTES　... or so「…くらい」　likewise「同様に」　associate A with B「A を B に結びつけて考える」
be confined to ...「…に限定される」　mainstream culture「主流の文化」
embrace「…を採り入れる」　as for ...「…について言えば」
behavioral「行動の」　Muji「無印良品」

Vocabulary Check

空所に適語を記入して、Analysis 本文中の下線を引いた単語や語句の意味を完成させましょう。

① 文化の（　　　　　　　）　　　　　⑥（　　　　　　　　　）

②（　　　　　　　　）経験　　　　　⑦（　　　　　　　　）

③（　　　　　　　　）待つ　　　　　⑧（　　　　　　　　）

④ 大幅な（　　　　　　）　　　　　　⑨（　　　　　　　　）

⑤（　　　　　　　　　）　　　　　　⑩ 世界を（　　　　　　　　）

Comprehension

各パラグラフの主題文が ███████ で示されています。空所に適語を記入して、それぞれの主題文の訳を完成させましょう。その後、各パラグラフに関する設問に答えましょう。

Paragraph❶

主題文の訳：しかしながら、（　　　　　　　　　　）くらいの間、（　　　　　　　　　　　　　　　）が非常に高くなっている。

📝 an explosion of interest の具体的な現象として述べられている以下の例について、日本語でまとめましょう。

日本料理店：_____

すし：_____

北海道：_____

Paragraph❷

主題文の訳：こうした（　　　　　　　　　　　　　　　　）は食品だけに限ったことではない。

📝 本文の内容に合うように、次の英文の空所に適する単語を記入しましょう。

1. The words, "manga," "anime" and "emoji" now (　　　　　　　　) in English.

2. Manga, anime and emoji are very (　　　　　　　　) in the world, and they have become part of mainstream culture in many countries.

Paragraph❸

主題文の訳：興味深いことに、これらの日本文化の輸出は（　　　　　　　　　　　　　）に吸収され、（　　　　　　　　　　　　　　　）適合されている。

 アメリカのカリフォルニアロールと日本のカレーの共通点を日本語で述べましょう。

_____

Paragraph❹

主題文の訳：ごく最近、（　　　　　　　　　　　　　）は食品やアニメやマンガのような（　　　　　　　）を超え、（　　　　　　　　　　　　　　　）まで拡大している。

 次の例に関して、さらなる日本文化の輸出拡大の表れといえる状況を日本語でまとめましょう。

ポケモン：_____

ユニクロと無印良品：_____

✓ Grammar Check ｜ 文と文をつないで副詞節をつくる接続詞

I got up at seven this morning.
It was raining then.

上の２つの文を１つにするには、接続詞 when を用いて、次のようにします。

When I got up at seven, it was raining.

このように２つの文をつなぐ接続詞には他に、if, unless, before, after, though, while, since などがあり、こうした接続詞で導かれる文はもう一方の文を修飾する役割をし、副詞の働きをするので副詞節と呼ばれます。

 次の英文は Analysis 本文からの抜粋です。下線部に注意して、訳を完成させましょう。

<u>While it may be unlikely that a Japanese theme park conquers the world</u>, it seems like Japan's culture has already had a big international influence and will continue to grow in the future.

訳：（

　　　　　　　　　）、日本文化はすでに大きな国際的影響力を持っていて、今後も成長し続けるように思われる。

●Report Completion

巻末 p. 104 にある **Report 2** の **Ⅲ** 〜 **Ⅴ** に答えましょう。

✎ Interview in Future Japan

◀》 07

福岡のジャパニメでアメリカ人観光客がインタビューを受けています。その音声を聴き、次の英文が
インタビューの内容に合っていれば True に、合っていなければ False に ✔ を入れましょう。

1. The American happened to find Japanime while traveling in Japan.　□ True □ False

2. The American says the storyline of Japanese anime is very
interesting.　□ True □ False

3. The American thinks anime is different from animation.　□ True □ False

Writing Composition

Analysis 本文中の [　　] 内の表現を使って、次の日本語の意味を表す英文を完成させましょう。

1. 私はこの街ですでに 10 軒くらいの日本料理店を見つけた。[or so]

I (　　　　　　　) (　　　　　　　) (　　　　　　　) 10 (　　　　　　　)

(　　　　　　　) Japanese restaurants in this town.

2. 日本のアニメを江戸時代の浮世絵と関連づける評論家がいる。[associate A with B]

(　　　　　　　) critics (　　　　　　　) (　　　　　　　) (　　　　　　　)

(　　　　　　　) *ukiyoe* in Edo Period.

3. マンガの人気は子どもだけに限定されない。[be confined to]

The (　　　　　　　) of manga is (　　　　　　　) (　　　　　　　)

(　　　　　　　) (　　　　　　　).

4. 日本の食文化について言えば、醤油は世界中のスーパーマーケットで売られている。

[as for]

(　　　　　　　) (　　　　　　　) (　　　　　　　) (　　　　　　　)

(　　　　　　　), soy sauce (　　　　　　　) (　　　　　　　) at supermarkets all

over the world.

5. 寿司は日本の伝統的な食べ物であるが、今では多くの国で食べられている。[while]

(　　　　　　　) sushi is (　　　　　　　) (　　　　　　　) (　　　　　　　), now

(　　　　　　　) (　　　　　　　) (　　　　　　　) in many countries.

Japan's unemployment hits 30% as AI advances

The Labor Department <u>announced</u> today that the <u>unemployment</u> level in Japan has reached 30%, a new record high. Department spokesperson, Goh Watanabe, also projected that the jobless totals may reach as high as 50% by 2050 as <u>automation</u>, robots and AI continue to take the place of human workers. He <u>noted</u> that all buses, taxis and delivery <u>vehicles</u> in Tokyo are now driverless. Another <u>occupation</u> hard hit by AI was health care. Watanabe claimed that fewer family doctors were needed because <u>diagnosis</u> and treatment of diseases are now mostly performed by computers. "After a simple blood test, a computer can <u>analyze</u> the results and automatically <u>recommend</u> a treatment. It seems that occupations at all levels are being <u>affected</u>," he said.

 この記事のヘッドラインを日本語にしましょう。

_____

Vocabulary Check

次の意味に該当するものを記事中の下線を引いた単語から抜き出しましょう。ただし、動詞は原形で答えましょう。

1. 職業 _____
2. 失業 _____
3. …を分析する _____
4. …に特に言及する _____
5. 乗り物 _____
6. 自動化 _____
7. 診断 _____
8. …を発表する _____
9. 影響を与える _____
10. …を勧める _____

Comprehension

空所に適語を記入して、記事の要旨を完成させましょう。

労働省の発表によれば、(　　　　　　　　　　　　　　　　　　　　　　　　　　　　)。
今後も自動化、ロボット、AI が (　　　　　　　　　　　　　　　)、2050 年までには
失業率は 50 パーセントに達するかもしれない。

Report Completion

巻末 p. 105 にある **Report 3** の Ⅰ と Ⅱ に答えましょう。

Analysis

1   At the beginning of the 20th century, the blacksmith, or horseshoe maker, was ① <u>a</u>   01
<u>common occupation</u>. However, because ② <u>cars replaced horses</u> as a means of travel, the   02
blacksmith gradually disappeared. <u>Presently, we are in ③ a similar shift, although the</u>   03
<u>changes we are experiencing today may be far more dramatic.</u> Unlike past eras of   04
change, such as the Renaissance or the Industrial Revolution, ④ <u>the present era</u> could   05
make many workers redundant. Many of these redundancies, such as the change to self-   06
driving vehicles, or robotic chefs, will appear before 2040. In fact, several cities are   07
already testing driverless vehicles.   08

2   <u>Similarly, there are many other occupations that may soon disappear.</u> As online   09
shopping grows in popularity, there will be less need for salespeople. When an app   10
knows your ⑤ <u>personal preferences</u> based on ⑥ <u>previous purchases</u>, there is little need for   11
a salesperson to help you. As for payment, cashiers are already being replaced in many   12
supermarkets by self-checkout machines. In fact, many activities that we perform   13
online, such as buying books and travel, or doing our banking, are ⑦ <u>reducing the need</u>   14
for human labor.   15

3   Therefore, what are the occupations that are most likely to be in demand in the   16
future? This is a very difficult question because even jobs that require creativity may   17
disappear. Amazingly, computers are now able to create art, and compose music and   18
novels. So it seems like there are no professions that are ⑧ <u>guaranteed to exist</u> in the   19
future, except perhaps computer programming.   20

4   However, ⑨ <u>predicting the future</u> is often called a fool's game. No one really knows   21
what jobs will appear and disappear. Some predictions say that many new jobs will be   22
created just like when car mechanics replaced the blacksmith. Others say people will   23
always prefer human contact over robots or computers. Whatever the case, young   24
people planning their future careers need to carefully watch trends and be ⑩ <u>flexible</u>   25
<u>about plans</u> for the rest of their lives.   26

NOTES   blacksmith「鍛冶屋」 unlike「…とは違って」 redundant「過多の」 based on ...「…に基づいた」
be likely to *be*「…になりそうだ」 in demand「需要がある」 it seems like ...「…であるようだ」
whatever the case「どうであれ」

24

Vocabulary Check

空所に適語を記入して、Analysis 本文中の下線を引いた語句の意味を完成させましょう。

①（　　　　　　　）職業
②車が馬に（　　　　　　　　　　）
③（　　　　　　　）変化
④（　　　　）時代
⑤個人の（　　　　）
⑥以前の（　　　　）
⑦必要性を（　　　　　　　）
⑧存在することを（　　　　　　　）
⑨未来を（　　　　　　　）
⑩計画について（　　　　　）

Comprehension

各パラグラフの主題文が　　　　で示されています。空所に適語を記入して、それぞれの主題文の訳を完成させましょう。その後、各パラグラフに関する設問に答えましょう。

Paragraph❶

主題文の訳： 今日（こんにち）（　　　　　　　　　　　　　）のほうがはるかに劇的かもしれないが、
現在、私たちは（　　　　　　　　　　　　　）。

次の書き出しに続けて、筆者が主題文で波下線部のように述べている理由を完成させましょう。

ルネッサンスや産業革命とは違って、＿＿＿＿＿＿＿＿＿＿＿＿＿＿＿＿＿＿＿＿

＿＿＿＿＿＿＿＿＿＿＿＿＿＿＿＿＿＿＿＿＿＿＿＿＿＿＿＿＿＿＿＿＿＿＿＿。

Paragraph❷

主題文の訳： 同様に、（　　　　　　　　　　　　　　　　）多くの他の職業がある。

筆者が将来なくなると予想している職種を本文から２つ抜き出し、その根拠を日本語で答えましょう。

職　種	根　拠

Paragraph❸

主題文の訳：だから、たぶん（ 　　　　　　　　　　　　　　　 ）を除くと、将来（ 　　　　　　　　　　 ）はなさそうだ。

📝 次の英文は筆者が主題文でこのように述べている理由です。空所に適する単語を記入しましょう。

Computers are even able to perform jobs that (　　　　　) (　　　　).

Paragraph❹

主題文の訳：どうであれ、（ 　　　　　　　　　　　　　　 ）若者は注意深く（ 　　　　　　 ）、残りの人生の計画について（ 　　　　　　 ）必要がある。

📝 本文で述べられている職に関する将来の予測を2つ、日本語で答えましょう。

・ _____

・ _____

✅ Grammar Check　a little と little

There is a little juice in the glass.
There is little juice in the glass.

上の2つの文の表現上の違いは little の前の a の有無だけですが、その意味合いは大きく異なります。前者は「グラスに少しジュースがある」で、後者は「グラスにほとんどジュースがない」となり、little の前に a が無い場合は否定的な意味になります。数えられる名詞に使う a few と few も同様です。

📝 次の英文は Analysis 本文からの抜粋です。下線部に注意して、訳を完成させしましょう。

When an app knows your personal preferences based on previous purchases, there is <u>little</u> need for a salesperson to help you.

訳：アプリが（ 　　　　　　　　　　　　　　　　　 ）をわかっていると、販売員が（ 　　　　　　　　　　　　　　　 ）。

⬤ Report Completion

巻末 p. 106 にある **Report 3** の Ⅲ 〜 Ⅴ に答えましょう。

🖉 Interview in Future Japan 🔊 10

日本のスーパーマーケットで買い物客がインタビューを受けています。その音声を聴き、次の英文が
インタビューの内容に合っていれば True に、合っていなければ False に ✓ を入れましょう。

1. Smile supermarket has no human cashiers now. □ True □ False

2. The customer was completely satisfied with the self-checkout □ True □ False
   machine.

3. The customer will never shop at the store again. □ True □ False

Writing Composition

Analysis 本文中の [   ] 内の表現を使って、次の日本語の意味を表す英文を完成させましょう。

1. 今の時代とは違って、私が子どもの頃は携帯電話を持っている人はほとんどいなかった。

   [unlike]

   (   ) the (   ) (   ), when I was a child,
   (   ) (   ) had their own cell phones.

2. コンピュータは血液検査に基づいた治療法を推奨することができる。[based on]
   Computers can (   ) a treatment (   ) (   ) a
   (   ) (   ).

3. 医療では、ますます多くの外国人労働者の需要があるだろう。[in demand]
   In (   ) (   ), more and more foreign workers
   (   ) (   ) (   ) (   ).

4. そのスーパーマーケットでは、レジ係が自動精算機に取って代わられたようだ。

   [it seems like]

   At the supermarket, (   ) (   ) (   ) cashiers
   have (   ) (   ) by self-checkout machines.

5. 誰も未来を正確に予測できないが、どうであれ私たちは予測不能な未来に備える必要がある。

   [whatever the case]

   No one (   ) (   ) the future accurately, but
   (   ) (   ) (   ), we still need to
   (   ) (   ) an unpredictable future.

Burger McMoss sells its last hamburger made of real beef

Yesterday, the fast food chain, McMoss sold its final hamburger made with beef. Starting today, the restaurant will no longer make its hamburger patties from meat. Instead, they will be made of <u>soybeans</u> and <u>peas</u> along with vegetable oils and other <u>ingredients</u>. Keiko Tanaka, manager of one of the chain's restaurants in Harajuku explains: "Over the past several years, we have been <u>experimenting</u> with <u>various</u> types of vegetable patties and we found our customers actually preferred the non-meat burgers. The taste and <u>texture</u> kept getting closer to real beef and <u>eventually</u> customers started to request the vegetarian burger more than the real meat one. We were really <u>pleased</u> about this because the vegetable patty is <u>quite a bit</u> cheaper than the beef one so we can pass on the <u>savings</u> to our customers."

 この記事のヘッドラインを日本語にしましょう。

Vocabulary Check

次の意味に該当するものを記事中の下線を引いた単語または語句から抜き出しましょう。ただし、動詞は原形で答えましょう。

1. 大豆 _____
2. 様々な _____
3. 実験する _____
4. 節約分 _____
5. エンドウ豆 _____
6. やがて _____
7. 舌ざわり _____
8. 食材 _____
9. 喜んで _____
10. かなり _____

Comprehension

空所に適語を記入して、記事の要旨を完成させましょう。

> マックモスは本日で（　　　　　　　　　　　　　　）を終了し、代わりに（　　　　　　　　）を使う。原宿店の責任者によれば、ここ数年にわたって（　　　　　　　　　　　　）を試し、（　　　　　　　　　　　　　　　　　　）ことがわかったという。野菜のパテはかなり安いので、その節約分を（　　　　　　　　　　　　　　）ということだ。

Report Completion

巻末 p. 107 にある **Report 4** の **I** と **II** に答えましょう。

Analysis

1   Although the traditional Japanese diet of rice and fish is known to be very healthy, in recent years, Japanese are eating more meat, especially chicken and pork. This type of diet may be less healthy because ①meat consumption is associated with ②heart disease and certain types of cancer. Meat, as a ③food source, is also known to damage the environment much more than vegetables. Therefore, Japan ④shares some responsibility because it is the largest meat-importing country in the world.

2   Japan actually has a long tradition of vegetarian cuisine. *Shojin ryori,* vegetarian dishes served in Buddhist temples, was introduced in Japan in the 13th century. Instead of bonito flakes, for example, seaweed is used to make miso soup.

3   There are a few reasons why vegetarian food may become more popular in the future. With ⑤a growing concern about the environment, younger Japanese may want to avoid ⑥contributing to climate change. Just as one example, cows produce methane gas which is a major contributor to global warming. Then there is also the treatment of farm animals. Animal rights groups have ⑦criticized the ⑧cruel living conditions experienced by livestock. On many chicken farms, for example, the birds are kept in tiny cages their whole lives without being able to spread their wings. Another concern is the amount of land that has been cleared simply to grow animal feed. Vast hectares of the Amazon rainforest have been cut down just to grow soybeans to be fed to farm animals and farmed fish.

4   Perhaps ⑨the long-term solution is "clean meat." This meat has been grown from the cells of a real animal in a laboratory so it ⑩tastes almost exactly like meat; however, no animal has to be killed. In 2013, the first hamburger made of clean meat was produced and eaten. Although there are still many challenges to producing clean meat on a mass scale, it could become our main source of meat in the future.

01
02
03
04
05
06
07
08
09
10
11
12
13
14
15
16
17
18
19
20
21
22
23
24

NOTES less healthy 「より健康的でない」（less は「より…でない」という否定の意味を表す比較表現。
＜less ＋形容詞／副詞＞の形でしばしば使われる）　bonito flakes 「かつお節」
seaweed 「昆布」　methane gas 「メタンガス」　contributor 「貢献するもの」
livestock 「家畜」　hectare 「ヘクタール」　farmed fish 「養殖魚」
on a mass scale 「大規模に」

Vocabulary Check

空所に適語を記入して、Analysis 本文中の下線を引いた単語や語句の意味を完成させましょう。

① 肉の（　　　　　　）

② 心臓の（　　　　　　）

③ 食糧（　　　　　）

④ （　　　　　　　　　　　）共有する

⑤ 増大する（　　　　　）

⑥ 気候変動に（　　　　　　　　）こと

⑦ （　　　　　　　）

⑧ （　　　　　　　　　）生活状況

⑨ 長期的な（　　　　　　　）

⑩ （　　　　　　　）

Comprehension

各パラグラフの主題文が ▨▨▨▨▨ で示されています。空所に適語を記入して、それぞれの主題文の訳を完成させましょう。その後、各パラグラフに関する設問に答えましょう。

Paragraph❶

主題文の訳：（　　　　　　　　　　　　　　　　　）はとても健康的であるとして知られているが、近年、日本人は（　　　　　　　　　　　　　　　　　）。

✎ 次の英文が本文の内容と合うように、空所に適する単語を記入しましょう。

1. A diet of rice and fish is (　　　　　) for your health than that of meat.
2. Eating vegetables damages the environment (　　　　　) than eating meat.
3. Japan imports (　　　　　) meat than any other country in the world.

Paragraph❷

主題文の訳：実際、日本には（　　　　　　　　　　　　　　　　　　　）。

✎ 次の英文は精進料理についての説明です。本文に合うように、空所に適する単語を記入しましょう。

In the 13th century, (　　　　　　　) (　　　　　　　) started to (　　　　　　　) *shojin ryori*, which is made of (　　　　　　　) without any meat.

Paragraph❸

主題文の訳：（　　　　　　　　　　　　　　　　　　　　　　　　　　　） という理由がいくつかある。

✐　主題文の中の a few reasons について、次のキーワードごとに日本語で説明しましょう。

the environment: _____

livestock: _____

cleared land: _____

Paragraph❹

主題文の訳：（　　　　　　　　　　　　　　　　　　　） についてはまだ多くの課題があ
　　　　　　るが、将来（　　　　　　　　　　　　　　） かもしれない。

✐　clean meat について、次の質問に英語で答えましょう。

1. Is the meat produced on a farm? — _____

2. Is the taste similar to that of real meat? — _____

3. Are there any people who have eaten clean meat? — _____

✓ Grammar Check　過去分詞の形容詞的用法

受動態（be 動詞＋過去分詞）や、現在完了形（have/has ＋過去分詞）で用いられる過去分詞には、名詞を修飾する形容詞の働きもあります。たとえば、a broken glass（割られたグラス ⇒ 割れたグラス）は broken が受け身の意味合いで glass を修飾しており、fallen leaves（落ちてしまった葉 ⇒ 落ち葉）といえば、fallen が完了の意味合いで leaves を修飾しています。なお、このような過去分詞を他の語と一緒に句の形で使うときは、a glass broken by someone のように修飾する名詞の後ろに置きます。

✐　次の英文は Analysis 本文からの抜粋です。下線部に注意して、訳を完成させしましょう。

In 2013, <u>the first hamburger made of clean meat</u> was produced and eaten.

訳：2013 年に （　　　　　　　　　　　　　　　　　　　　） が生産され、
　　食べられた。

● Report Completion

巻末 p. 108 にある **Report 4** の **III** ～ **V** に答えましょう。

✎ Interview in Future Japan　　　　　🔊 13

マックモスから出てきた客がインタビューを受けています。その音声を聴き、次の英文がインタビューの内容に合っていれば True に、合っていなければ False に ✔ を入れましょう。

1. The customer tried the vegeburger alone.　　　　　□ True □ False

2. The customer says the taste of vegeburgers is quite different from　□ True □ False
that of beef burgers.

3. The customer doesn't want to hurt animals.　　　　　□ True □ False

▧ Writing Composition

記事中または Analysis 本文中の [　　] 内の表現を使って、次の日本語の意味を表す英文を完成させましょう。

1. 日本では、野菜は牛肉よりかなり安い。[quite a bit]

In Japan, (　　　　　) (　　　　　　) (　　　　　　) (　　　　　　)
(　　　　　) (　　　　　　) than beef.

2. 肉は野菜より健康的でないという人が多い。[less]

(　　　　　) (　　　　　) (　　　　　　) that meat (　　　　　)
(　　　　　) (　　　　　) (　　　　　　) vegetables.

3. 彼女がベジタリアンになった理由はいくつかある。[a few reasons why]

(　　　　　) (　　　　　　) a few (　　　　　) (　　　　　　) she
(　　　　　) (　　　　　　) a vegetarian.

4. このレストランで出されるアイスクリームは大豆から作られている。[名詞＋過去分詞]

The ice cream (　　　　　) (　　　　　) (　　　　　)
(　　　　　) is (　　　　　　) from soybeans.

5. 私たちは地球温暖化に寄与するものを買うことを避けるべきだ。[avoid *doing*]

(　　　　　) (　　　　　　) (　　　　　　) (　　　　　　) something
that will contribute to (　　　　　) (　　　　　　).

Shinkansen takes its last passengers

Japan's famous bullet train will carry its last passengers later today from Tokyo to Kagoshima with the opening of the Hyperloop scheduled for tomorrow, April 25, just in time for Golden Week. Tickets for the Shinkansen's final trip sold out over six months ago in late 2059, as fans were willing to pay triple the regular price. Replacing the bullet train, the new Hyperloop will take passengers four times faster at half the price to the same destinations where the present Shinkansen goes. A spokesperson for the new service said that travel time from Tokyo to Sapporo will take 70 minutes and Osaka to Fukuoka will take 40 minutes.

 この記事のヘッドラインを日本語にしましょう。

Vocabulary Check

次の意味に該当するものを記事中の下線を引いた単語または語句から抜き出しましょう。ただし、動詞は原形で答えましょう。

1. 3倍の　　　＿＿＿＿＿＿＿＿＿＿＿＿＿＿＿＿＿
2. 新幹線　　　＿＿＿＿＿＿＿＿＿＿＿＿＿＿＿＿＿
3. 現在の　　　＿＿＿＿＿＿＿＿＿＿＿＿＿＿＿＿＿
4. 進んで…する　＿＿＿＿＿＿＿＿＿＿＿＿＿＿＿＿＿
5. 目的地　　　＿＿＿＿＿＿＿＿＿＿＿＿＿＿＿＿＿
6. …に間に合って　＿＿＿＿＿＿＿＿＿＿＿＿＿＿＿＿＿
7. 乗客　　　　＿＿＿＿＿＿＿＿＿＿＿＿＿＿＿＿＿
8. 通常の　　　＿＿＿＿＿＿＿＿＿＿＿＿＿＿＿＿＿
9. …を運ぶ　　＿＿＿＿＿＿＿＿＿＿＿＿＿＿＿＿＿
10. 予定された　＿＿＿＿＿＿＿＿＿＿＿＿＿＿＿＿＿

Comprehension

空所に適語を記入して、記事の要旨を完成させましょう。

（　　　　　　　　　　　　　　）を翌日に控え、新幹線は東京から鹿児島へ（　　　　　　　　）予定だ。新幹線の最終便の乗車券は半年以上前に売り切れ、（　　　　）の値が付いた。ハイパーループは新幹線の（　　　　　　）の速さ、（　　　　　）の運賃で乗客を運ぶことになる。

Report Completion

巻末 p. 109 にある **Report 5** の **I** と **II** に答えましょう。

Analysis

🔊 15

1　Presently there are two ways to travel between major cities: on airplanes and the bullet train. However, both are inefficient ways to move people. Heavy airplanes have to rise to about 10 kilometers into the sky carrying people and ①fuel. Then once near their destination, they ②descend back to land. Going from point A to B like this is very inefficient in terms of both fuel and time. As for the bullet train, it cannot go much faster than 300 kilometers per hour because it has to stay on its rails and also push through air. It also uses up a lot of land.

2　The Hyperloop has the ③potential to solve these problems because passengers would travel underground in capsules that shoot through a tube. Once the capsules and the tubes are built, the cost to ④operate the system would be much lower than ⑤other types of transport. Pushing a capsule through a vacuum tube using magnets requires much less energy because there is no air friction. Also, ⑥labor costs would be low because the capsules would not require a pilot. Although the Hyperloop may seem like science fiction, there is already a trial version in the United States. Presently, the top speed has reached only 400 kilometers an hour, but ⑦the target speed is 1,200.

3　Of course, there are many technical challenges to ⑧overcome. For example, sudden acceleration can be very uncomfortable for the human brain. Sudden changes in speed could cause passengers to pass out. Also, when traveling so quickly, any small bumps could be quite ⑨frightening.

4　However, there is a great incentive for companies to provide cheap and fast transportation. Also, because airplanes are a big contributor to global warming, there is a need to develop a system that is energy efficient. Presently, our best option is to fly between cities, which is neither cheap nor environmentally ⑩sustainable. Thus, the Hyperloop has the potential to change the way we travel.

01 02 03 04 05 06 07 08 09 10 11 12 13 14 15 16 17 18 19 20 21 22 23 24

NOTES once「いったん…すると」（3行目と9行目の once はどちらも接続詞。3行目のものは＜主語＋述語＞が省略されている）　in terms of ...「…の点からすると」　as for ...「…については」
vacuum tube「真空管」　air friction「空気摩擦」　acceleration「加速」　pass out「意識を失う」
bump「揺れ」　incentive「動機」　energy efficient「エネルギー効率の良い」
neither A nor B「A でも B でもない」

Vocabulary Check

空所に適語を記入して、Analysis 本文中の下線を引いた単語や語句の意味を完成させましょう。

① (　　　　　　　　　　) 　　　　　　　　　⑥ (　　　　　　　　　　)

② 陸へとまた (　　　　　　) 　　　　　　　　⑦ (　　　　　) の速度

③ (　　　　　　　　　　) 　　　　　　　　　⑧ (　　　　　　　　　　)

④ そのシステムを (　　　　　　　) 　　　　　⑨ (　　　　　　　　　　)

⑤ その他の (　　　　　　　) 　　　　　　　　⑩ (　　　　　　　　　　)

Comprehension

各パラグラフの主題文が ░░░░ で示されています。空所に適語を記入して、それぞれの主題文の訳を完成させましょう。その後、各パラグラフに関する設問に答えましょう。

Paragraph❶

主題文の訳：現在、(　　　　　　　　　　　　　　) には 2 つの方法がある。(　　　　　) と (　　　　　) だ。しかし、どちらも (　　　　　　　　　　　　　　) である。

🖊 主題文のように筆者が述べている理由を、次の 2 つの例について日本語でまとめましょう。

飛行機：＿＿＿＿＿＿＿＿＿＿＿＿＿＿＿＿＿＿＿＿＿＿＿＿＿＿＿＿＿＿＿＿＿

新幹線：＿＿＿＿＿＿＿＿＿＿＿＿＿＿＿＿＿＿＿＿＿＿＿＿＿＿＿＿＿＿＿＿＿

Paragraph❷

主題文の訳：乗客は (　　　　　　　　　　　　　　　　　　) ので、ハイパーループは (　　　　　　　　　　　　　　) 可能性を有している。

🖊 次の英文はハイパーループの利点を述べたものです。本文に合うように、空所に適する単語を記入しましょう。

1. The Hyperloop is operated at a much (　　　　　　　) cost than any other form of transport.

2. The Hyperloop needs much less (　　　　　　　) because it moves without any air friction.

3. The Hyperloop needs no pilots, so (　　　　　) (　　　　　　　) would be low.

Paragraph❸

主題文の訳：もちろん、（　　　　　　　　　　　　　　　　　　　　　　　）は多くある。

 ハイパールーフの問題点について、次の質問に英語で答えましょう。

1. What can be uncomfortable for the human brain? ― _____

2. What might cause some passengers to pass out? ― _____

Paragraph❹

主題文の訳：従って、ハイパールーフは（　　　　　　　　　　　　　　　　　　　　）
　　　　　　　を有しているのだ。

 将来の輸送手段としてハイパールーフが飛行機より有望であることを示す単語やフレーズを本文から 3 つ抜き出しましょう。

・_____　　・_____　　・_____

✓ Grammar Check　｜　前の名詞を修飾する不定詞

I have a lot of books.（私はたくさんの本を持っている）

上の文の books の後ろに to read が付けると、次のようになります。

I have a lot of books to read.

この文は「私には読むべき本がたくさんある」という意味になり、to read は直前の名詞 books を修飾していることから、不定詞の形容詞的用法と呼ばれます。では、I had money に to buy a new smartphone を続けるとどうなりますか。「私は新しいスマートフォンを買うためのお金を持っていた」という意味になり、to 以下は名詞 money を修飾します。

 次の英文は Analysis 本文からの抜粋です。下線部に注意して、訳を完成させしましょう。

Also, because airplanes are a big contributor to global warming, there is <u>a need to develop</u> a system that is energy efficient.

訳：また、飛行機は地球温暖化に大きな影響を与えるので、（
　　　　　　　　　　　　　　　　　　　　　）がある。

● Report Completion

巻末 p. 110 にある **Report 5** の **Ⅲ** ～ **Ⅴ** に答えましょう。

✎ Interview in Future Japan 🔊 16

ハイパーループを体験したばかりの乗客がインタビューを受けています。その音声を聴き、次の英文がインタビューの内容に合っていれば True に、合っていなければ False に ✓ を入れましょう。

1. The passenger took the Hyperloop from Osaka to Tokyo. ☐ True ☐ False

2. The passenger wishes to see the scenery from the window. ☐ True ☐ False

3. The passenger is living alone in Osaka now. ☐ True ☐ False

Writing Composition

記事中または Analysis 本文中の ［　］内の表現を使って、次の日本語の意味を表す英文を完成させましょう。

1. どこに行くにも、私は車を使わないで進んで公共の輸送機関を利用する。

［be willing to *do*］

Wherever I go, I (　　　　　) (　　　　　) (　　　　　) (　　　　　)
public transportation (　　　　　) using my car.

2. タクシーを拾ったほうがいいですね。そうしないと開会式に間に合いません。

［in time for］

We'd better take a taxi or else we won't (　　　　　) (　　　　　)
(　　　　　) (　　　　　) the opening ceremony.

3. いったんセキュリティチェックを受けたら、空港の外へ出ることはできません。

［once ＋主語＋述語］

(　　　　　) (　　　　　) undergo the (　　　　　) (　　　　　),
you cannot (　　　　　) (　　　　　) (　　　　　) the airport.

4. 私たちは地球温暖化に与える影響の点から、未来の輸送について考えるべきだ。

［in terms of］

We should think about our (　　　　　) (　　　　　) (　　　　　)
(　　　　　) (　　　　　) its effects on (　　　　　) (　　　　　).

5. 環境問題については、克服すべき課題がたくさんある。［名詞＋不定詞］

(　　　　　) (　　　　　) (　　　　　) issues, we have a lot of
(　　　　　) (　　　　　) (　　　　　).

English removed from the Center Test

The Ministry of Education, Culture, Sports, Science and Technology (MEXT) recommended today that English be <u>removed</u> from all university entrance exams as of 2040. The reason, according to <u>recent</u> discussions at the Ministry, is the <u>perfection</u> of computer translation services. Now, any text that is written or spoken in Japanese and then entered into hand-held mobile <u>devices</u> can be <u>instantly</u> and perfectly translated into English. On the Center Test, English will be replaced by computer coding. Ministry spokesperson, Naomi Oka, <u>explained</u> that MEXT had been <u>considering</u> the move for several years as computer translation continually improved. Oka added, "<u>for the time being</u>, Chinese will be the only <u>required</u> foreign language on the test, but because computer translations between Japanese and Chinese are also <u>close to</u> perfect, it may also be removed from the test in the near future."

 この記事のヘッドラインを日本語にしましょう。

Vocabulary Check

次の意味に該当するものを記事中の下線を引いた単語または語句から抜き出しましょう。ただし、動詞は原形で答えましょう。

1. 装置　　　　　_____
2. …を説明する　_____
3. …を除外する　_____
4. 当分の間　　　_____
5. 最近の　　　　_____
6. …を検討する　_____
7. …に近い　　　_____
8. 完璧さ　　　　_____
9. 必須の　　　　_____
10. 即座に　　　　_____

Comprehension

空所に適語を記入して、記事の要旨を完成させましょう。

> コンピュータの翻訳サービスの完璧な完成度に伴い、文部科学省は 2040 年度より
> （　　　　　　　　　　　　　　　　　　　　　）を勧告した。英語に代わって（　　　　
> 　　　）がセンター試験に採用される見通しである。当面は中国語だけ
> が（　　　　　　　）であるが、近い将来に中国語も（
> 　　　　）かもしれないということだ。

Report Completion

巻末 p. 111 にある **Report 6** の **I** と **II** に答えましょう。

Analysis

1   Until recently, computer translators produced very poor results, especially when translating into English from languages such as Japanese and Chinese, which are quite ① linguistically ② distant from English. Often the translations made no sense at all. However, recently, computer translation has become much ③ more accurate. Now, computers are programmed to make sense of a whole sentence using a bank of previously human translated text. This method is much more accurate than the old way, which translated a few words, without taking the whole context into account.

2   Ironically, the great improvement in machine translation arrives at a time when English is being introduced at a younger age in Japan's primary schools. Japan has actually been quite slow to introduce English into primary school ④ compared to other Asian countries such as China, Taiwan and Korea. However, with perfect machine translation possibly arriving within ⑤ the next decade, the question arises whether it is necessary to learn a foreign language. After all, to give ⑥ a parallel example, when the calculator was first introduced, people immediately ⑦ adopted it to perform ⑧ difficult calculations.

3   The likely reality is that people will continue to learn foreign languages, especially English and Chinese. This is because humans prefer to communicate face to face without a machine in between. No matter how good a translation is, it is normal for people to want to enjoy natural interaction using their own voices and ears. Then there is also the desire to challenge oneself.

4   However, it is also possible that there will be a shift in foreign language learning to speaking and listening skills. Because computer translators will be able to provide perfect translations of text, language teaching and learning may ⑨ focus on oral language, which will still be necessary for ⑩ human interaction. However, even that is not certain; translation glasses and earphones have already been invented.

NOTES   make sense「意味をなす」 no ... at all「まったく…ない」 bank「貯蔵所、ここではデータバンク」
take ... into account「…を考慮に入れる」 in between「中間に」
no matter how ...「いかに…であろうとも」

Vocabulary Check

空所に適語を記入して、Analysis 本文中の下線を引いた単語や語句の意味を完成させましょう。

① （　　　　　　　　　）　　　　　　　　⑥ （　　　　　　　　）例

② …から （　　　　　　　　）　　　　　　⑦ それを （　　　　　　　）

③ より （　　　　　　　）　　　　　　　　⑧ 難しい （　　　　　　　）

④ …と （　　　　　　　　）　　　　　　　⑨ 話し言葉に （　　　　　　　　）

⑤ 次の （　　　　　　　）　　　　　　　　⑩ 人の （　　　　　　　）

Comprehension

各パラグラフの主題文が　　　　　　　で示されています。空所に適語を記入して、それぞれの主題文の訳を完成させましょう。その後、各パラグラフに関する設問に答えましょう。

Paragraph❶

主題文の訳：この方式は （　　　　　　　　　　　　　　　　　　　　　） で、古いやり方では
（　　　　　　　　　　　　　　） せず、（　　　　　　　　　　　　　） のだった。

✎　空所に適語を記入して、従来の翻訳機と現代の翻訳機の特徴を日本語でまとめましょう。

従来の翻訳機： （　　　　　　　　　　　　） を考えずに （　　　　　　） を翻訳した
　　　　　　　→ （　　　　　　　　　　　　　　　　） が多かった。

現代の翻訳機： （　　　　　　　　　　　　　　　　　　　　　） を活用し
　　　　　　　て、（　　　　　　　　　　　　　　　　　） ようにコンピュータが
　　　　　　　プログラムされており、従来のものより （　　　　　　　） になった。

Paragraph❷

主題文の訳：しかし （　　　　　　　　　　　　　　　　　　　　　　　　　） という
　　　　　　状況にあって、（　　　　　　　　　　　　　） があるのかという疑問が生じる。

✎　電卓の導入のどのような点が、翻訳機の普及の a parallel example として該当しますか。日本語で答えましょう。

_____

_____

Paragraph❸

主題文の訳：現実的には人々は（　　　　　）を、特に（　　　　　　　）を（　　　　　）
そうである。

✎ 主題文のように筆者が述べている理由を2つ、日本語で答えましょう。

・_____

・_____

Paragraph❹

主題文の訳：しかしまた、（　　　　　　　　　　　　　　　　　　　　　　　　　）
があるかもしれない。

✎ Reading、Writing、Listening、Speaking の4技能のうち、下記の2つの発明品によって語
学学習の対象から除外される可能性があるものを書き出しましょう。

computer translators: _____

translation glasses and earphones: _____

✓ Grammar Check　補足説明をする関係代名詞 which

The sports car, **which** has a big scratch, was for sale with a big discount.

上の文中の which は前にある The sports car を受けていて、which 以下はその補足説明となっ
ています。日本語訳は「そのスポーツカーには大きな傷があり、大きく値引きされて売り出され
ていた」となります。では、次の文の場合はどうでしょうか。

I'm looking for a sports car **which** costs under one million yen.

この文は「私は 100 万円以下のスポーツカーを探している」という内容で、which 以下は補足説
明でなく、探しているスポーツカーの条件を限定しており、a sports car を修飾しています。

✎ 次の英文は Analysis 本文からの抜粋です。下線部に注意して、訳を完成させましょう。

Until recently, computer translators produced very poor results, especially when
translating into English from languages such as Japanese and Chinese, <u>which</u> are
quite linguistically distant from English.

訳：最近まで、特に日本語や中国語のような言語から英語に翻訳するときはコンピュータ
翻訳の結果はとてもお粗末なものだったが、それは（
　　　　　）からである。

● Report Completion

巻末 p. 112 にある **Report 6** の **III** ～ **V** に答えましょう。

✎ Interview in Future Japan
🔊 19

羽田空港の出発ロビーで利用客がインタビューを受けています。その音声を聴き、次の英文がインタビューの内容に合っていれば True に、合っていなければ False に ✔ を入れましょう。

1. The tourist has a lot of confidence in her English.　　　　□ True □ False

2. The smartphone will be very useful on her trip.　　　　□ True □ False

3. The tourist is worried about nothing.　　　　□ True □ False

● Writing Composition

Analysis 本文中の [　] 内の表現を使って、次の日本語の意味を表す英文を完成させましょう。

1. 彼が翻訳した英語の手紙は意味がわからない。[make sense]

The English letter (　　　　　　) (　　　　　　　　) does not (　　　　　　)
(　　　　　　).

2. 外国語を学ぶ必要はまったくないという人々もいる。[not ... at all]

Some people say that they (　　　　　　) (　　　　　　) (　　　　　　)
(　　　　　　) a foreign language (　　　　　　) (　　　　　　).

3. 大学の教員は高校教育を考慮しなければならない。[take ... into account]

University educators (　　　　　　) (　　　　　　) (　　　　　　)
(　　　　　　) education (　　　　　　) (　　　　　　).

4. 両国の大統領は間に通訳を伴って会話を楽しんだ。[in between]

(　　　　　　) of the two countries (　　　　　　) the (　　　　　　) with
an interpreter (　　　　　　) (　　　　　　).

5. どんなにスマートフォンが便利でも、何もかもできるわけではない。[no matter how ...]

(　　　　　) (　　　　　) (　　　　　) (　　　　　) a
smartphone is, it cannot (　　　　　) (　　　　　).

Passports no longer required for international travel

The Ministry of Foreign Affairs announced today that as of tomorrow, July 1, 2040, travelers will no longer need to carry a passport when traveling abroad. Via an international <u>agreement</u> arranged through the United Nations, all international travelers will now be <u>scanned</u> at <u>borders</u> using <u>biometrics</u>. Smart cameras will use <u>facial recognition</u> technology to <u>instantly</u> <u>gather</u> information on each traveler. The Minister of Foreign Affairs, Takae Sakuma, said, "We have been testing our system over the past five years and we feel sure that it is impossible to trick our cameras as we view travelers' faces from <u>dozens of</u> <u>angles</u>." Sakuma added, "Even if someone gets a <u>nose job</u> to trick our cameras, <u>alarm bells</u> will sound."

 この記事のヘッドラインを日本語にしましょう。

_____

Vocabulary Check

次の意味に該当するものを記事中の下線を引いた単語または語句から抜き出しましょう。ただし、動詞は原形で答えましょう。

1. 顔認証 _____
2. 合意 _____
3. 警報ベル _____
4. 即座に _____
5. …をスキャンする _____
6. 生体認証 _____
7. 国境（ここでは入国審査） _____
8. …を集める _____
9. 何十もの角度 _____
10. 鼻の整形手術 _____

Comprehension

空所に適語を記入して、記事の要旨を完成させましょう。

> 外務省は、2040 年 7 月 1 日をもって（
> ）
> と発表した。これは国連の国際的合意によるもので、旅行者は入国審査で（
> ）がなされる。外務省によると、（
> ）ので不正はできないということだ。

Report Completion

巻末 p. 113 にある **Report 7** の **I** と **II** に答えましょう。

Analysis

1   Over the past few years, travelers have ①<u>noticed</u> changes, especially at airports. Now ₀₁ they can check in for flights online and simply scan ②<u>boarding passes</u> on their ₀₂ smartphones at the departure gate. At some airports, passengers even ③<u>attach</u> their ₀₃ baggage tags onto their own luggage. However, this is just the beginning of an ₀₄ automated airport experience. ₀₅

2   Facial recognition is no longer new. Already the technology has been perfected. ₀₆ Using multiple angles, a digital profile that is unique to ④<u>each individual</u> is instantly ₀₇ ⑤<u>generated</u>. In the near future, this technology can be combined with one's personal ₀₈ information. Thus, one's face will serve the same function as a passport. Travelers will ₀₉ still need to make sure they have ⑥<u>secured proper visas</u>, but these will be linked to their ₁₀ faces. Instead of meeting human customs officers and airline check-in staff, there will ₁₁ only be cameras at borders and departure gates. It will be ⑦<u>completely seamless</u>. Your ₁₂ face will silently do all the work. Of course, there will be agents behind the scenes just ₁₃ to make sure. ₁₄

3   One of the most ⑧<u>annoying aspects</u> of traveling by air is the security check. ₁₅ Sometimes long queues form and travelers have to take off shoes and throw away their ₁₆ drinks. In the future, smart scans using medical technology will be able to instantly ₁₇ recognize dangerous materials. Again, the ⑨<u>human presence</u> will be minimal. ₁₈

4   We may think that our present system using QR codes on boarding passes and ₁₉ embedded security in our passports is very hi-tech. However, in the coming decades, ₂₀ perhaps passports full of stamps from different countries will be displayed in museums, ₂₁ and visitors will look at them and wonder about how ⑩<u>primitive</u> our system of ₂₂ controlling travel was. The automated airport should make your travel quicker and ₂₃ smoother. ₂₄

NOTES be combined with ...「…と結びつけられる」 thus「このようにして」 make sure ...「…を確かめる」
customs officer「税関係官」 agent「係員」 behind the scenes「見えないところで」
minimal「最小限の」 embedded「埋め込まれた」

Vocabulary Check

空所に適語を記入して、Analysis 本文中の下線を引いた単語や語句の意味を完成させましょう。

① (　　　　　　　)
② (　　　　　　　)
③ (　　　　　　　)
④ 各々の (　　　　)
⑤ (　　　　　　　)

⑥ 適切なビザを (　　　　　　)
⑦ 完全に (　　　　　　　)
⑧ (　　　　　　　　) 側面
⑨ 人間の (　　　　　)
⑩ (　　　　　　　)

Comprehension

各パラグラフの主題文が ▨▨▨▨ で示されています。空所に適語を記入して、それぞれの主題文の訳を完成させましょう。その後、各パラグラフに関する設問に答えましょう。

Paragraph ❶

主題文の訳：ここ数年にわたって、旅行者は (　　　　　　　　　　　　　　　　　　　)。

📝 最新型の空港を利用した人が次のように語っています。本文に合うように、空所に適語を記入しましょう。

"I didn't have to wait at the counter because I had already (　　　) (　　　) online. I (　　　) the baggage tag onto my luggage myself, then proceeded to the (　　　) (　　　). My boarding pass was scanned on my (　　　), so it was very smooth and quick."

Paragraph ❷

主題文の訳：(　　　　　　　　　　) 新しくない。

📝 空所に適語を記入して、顔認証の技術について整理しましょう。

現在	複数の角度を利用して、(　　　　　　　　　　　　　　) が作成される。
近い将来	現在の技術が (　　　　　　) と結び合わされる。 　→ 顔が (　　　　　　) の働きをする。 (　　　　) が顔と適合される。 　→ (　　　　　　　　　　) では人間の係官などは見当たらず、 (　　　　　) があるのみ。

Paragraph ❸

主題文の訳：ここでもまた、（ 　　　　　　　　　　　　　　　　　　　　　　　　　　　　　　　　　 ）だろう。

📝 セキュリティチェックに関する次の質問に英語で答えましょう。

1. Currently, what do passengers sometimes (or always) have to do at the security check?

— _____

2. In the near future, when you carry something dangerous, what kind of machine will recognize it?

— _____

Paragraph ❹

主題文の訳：（ 　　　　　　　　　　 ）は（ 　　　　　　　　　　　　　　　　　　　　　　　　　　 ）
　　　　　　 はずだ。

📝 将来、博物館で展示されると予想されるものに ✔ を入れましょう。

☐ boarding pass ☐ facial recognition camera ☐ luggage tag
☐ passport ☐ visa

✔ Grammar Check 　完了を表す現在完了形

＜have/has ＋動詞の過去分詞＞で、「…してしまった」という行為の完了を表すことができます。たとえば、I wrote a letter. は過去のある時点で「手紙を書いた」という事実を述べていますが、I have written a letter. は、もう「手紙を書いてしまった。だから手紙は書き終わっている」ということを伝えています。現在完了形は時の流れの中で現在と必ずつながっているのです。完了を表す現在完了形では、already、yet、just などの副詞がよく一緒に用いられます。

📝 次の英文は Analysis 本文からの抜粋です。下線部に注意して、訳を完成させしましょう。

Facial recognition is no longer new. Already the technology <u>has been perfected</u>.

訳：顔認証はもはや新しくはない。すでに（ 　　　　　　　　　　　　　　　　　　　　　 ）。

● Report Completion

巻末 p. 114 にある **Report 7** の **Ⅲ** ～ **Ⅴ** に答えましょう。

✎ Interview in Future Japan

🔊 22

自動化された関西国際空港の到着ロビーで利用客がインタビューを受けています。その音声を聴き、次の英文がインタビューの内容に合っていれば True に、合っていなければ False に ✓ を入れましょう。

1. The woman was not checked by any officers on the way. □ True □ False
2. The woman likes everything about automated airports. □ True □ False
3. The woman doesn't like to see Japanese customs officers. □ True □ False

Writing Composition

Analysis 本文中の [   ] 内の表現を使って、次の日本語の意味を表す英文を完成させましょう。

1. 空港で係官にパスポートを見せる必要はもはやない。[no longer]

You (   ) (   ) (   ) (   )
(   ) your passport to the officer (   ) (   )
(   ).

2. 空港の自動化は利用客の安全と結びつけられるべきだ。[be combined with]

The automation of airports (   ) (   ) (   )
(   ) the (   ) of (   ).

3. 私たちの旅を快適にするために、見えないところで多くの人々が働いてくれている。

[behind the scenes]

In order to (   ) (   ) (   ) (   ),
a lot of people (   ) (   ) (   ) (   )
(   ) (   ).

4. バッグに航空券が入れてあることを確かめなさい。[make sure]

(   ) (   ) that (   ) (   ) your air
ticket (   ) (   ) (   ) (   ).

5. 123 便はもうすでに離陸してしまったので、次の便に乗ります。[have/has+ 過去分詞]

Since flight 123 (   ) (   ) (   )
(   ), I will take (   ) (   ) (   ).

Eleven Mart reintroduces human staff

In a return to the past, Eleven Mart plans to <u>reintroduce</u> human staff to some of its convenience stores. The <u>trial</u> plan is scheduled to begin in five stores in Japan's biggest cities later next year or in 2042 at the latest. A spokesperson for the chain, Masao Mizushima, said the company noticed that customers preferred to have some human interaction when they made their purchases. Mizushima added, "<u>Competition</u> among convenience store chains is <u>intense</u>, and we are always looking for ways that we can do something unique to <u>attract</u> customers to our stores. We realized that if we had one staff member in our stores during the busy hours, our customers would <u>appreciate</u> it." The <u>innovation</u> comes eight years after human staff <u>completely</u> disappeared from convenience stores in 2032 due to the labor <u>shortage</u> <u>coupled</u> with new technology that allowed completely automated payment.

 この記事のヘッドラインを日本語にしましょう。

Vocabulary Check

次の意味に該当するものを記事中の下線を引いた単語から抜き出しましょう。ただし、動詞は原形で
答えましょう。

1. …を再導入する　　　_____

2. 刷新　　　_____

3. 競争　　　_____

4. …を高く評価する　　　_____

5. 不足　　　_____

6. 完全に　　　_____

7. 試行の　　　_____

8. …を引き寄せる　　　_____

9. 激しい　　　_____

10. 合わせる　　　_____

Comprehension

空所に適語を記入して、記事の要旨を完成させましょう。

> イレブンマートは主要都市の 5 店舗で、(
> 　　　　　　　) を計画。(　　　　　　　　　　　　　　　　　　　　　　　) を好む
> ということに気づいたイレブンマートは、他社との激しい競争の中、その試みによって
> (　　　　　　　　　　　) ことを期待している。

Report Completion

巻末 p. 115 にある **Report 8** の **I** と **II** に答えましょう。

Analysis

1   Two trends are now ①<u>growing in strength</u> that will have ②<u>a huge impact</u> on Japanese society: the declining population and ③<u>the spread of technology</u> to replace human labor. Although Japan has long experience with automated machines that replace humans, such as ATMs and vending machines, we are now beginning to experience a whole new level of automation.

2   One example of this new level is at the convenience store. A model that Japan could follow is Amazon's first supermarket in Seattle. In this store, customers enter through some gates similar to those at the entrance of a subway, and swipe their smartphone equipped with an Amazon app. After entering, customers simply put the items they want into their shopping bags. When customers choose items from shelves, sensors will automatically ④<u>add the price</u> to their bill. If they change their mind and place the product back on the shelf, the sensor will ⑤<u>deduct the amount</u>. When they ⑥<u>exit the store</u>, an electronic receipt is issued and payment is deducted from their credit card or ⑦<u>bank account</u> without any human contact.

3   How does it work? Hundreds of infra-red cameras in the ceiling help to ⑧<u>recognize you</u> so that when you take a product off the shelf, the system knows it is you. And because the system knows your personal preferences, it ⑨<u>makes suggestions</u> to you as you shop.

4   In the meantime, some Japanese convenience store chains are already testing a similar system, although only very late at night for the time being. As the labor shortage increases, Japanese companies will have to find creative ways to replace human staff. If humans ⑩<u>eventually disappear</u> from all Japanese convenience stores and supermarkets, then those stores that do reintroduce human staff could have some advantage.

NOTES   similar to ...「…に似ている」 equipped with ...「…を装備した」 change *one's* mind「考えを変える」
infra-red「赤外線の」 so that S + V「S が V するように」 in the meantime「一方」
for the time being「当分の間」

54

Vocabulary Check

空所に適語を記入して、Analysis 本文中の下線を引いた語句の意味を完成させましょう。

① （　　　　　　　） が増している

② 大きな （　　　　　　）

③ 科学技術の （　　　　　　　）

④ その価格を （　　　　　　）

⑤ その額を （　　　　　　）

⑥ その店を （　　　　　　　）

⑦ 銀行 （　　　　　　）

⑧ あなたを （　　　　　　　）

⑨ （　　　　　　） をする

⑩ 最終的に （　　　　　　　）

Comprehension

Analysis 本文の各パラグラフにおいて、その主題文（1 ～ 2 文）を抜き出しましょう。その後、各パラグラフに関する設問に答えましょう。

Paragraph❶

主題文：＿＿＿＿＿＿＿＿＿＿＿＿＿＿＿＿＿＿＿＿＿＿＿＿＿＿＿

＿＿＿＿＿＿＿＿＿＿＿＿＿＿＿＿＿＿＿＿＿＿＿＿＿＿＿＿＿＿

本文で述べられている日本社会の 2 つの傾向を日本語で答えましょう。

・＿＿＿＿＿＿＿＿＿＿＿＿＿　　・＿＿＿＿＿＿＿＿＿＿＿＿＿

Paragraph❷

主題文：＿＿＿＿＿＿＿＿＿＿＿＿＿＿＿＿＿＿＿＿＿＿＿＿＿＿＿

次の英文は、シアトルにある Amazon のスーパーマーケット 1 号店での買い物の仕方を説明したものです。空所に適する単語を記入しましょう。

Have you downloaded the Amazon app on your (① 　　　　　　　) yet? (② 　　　　　　　) your smartphone with the app on the screen when entering through the gate. In the store, just enjoy shopping! All you have to do is put the items you want into your bag. And then, please exit the store. There's no need to go to the cashier. An electronic (③ 　　　　　　　) is issued, and the payment is (④ 　　　　　　　) from your credit card or bank account. (⑤ 　　　　　　　) know what you have bought and have calculated the bill. It's quick and easy!

Paragraph❸

主題文： _____

📝 赤外線カメラの機能について、次の質問に英語で答えましょう。

1. Do infra-red cameras know who you are? — _____

2. If you take an item from the shelf, do the cameras know that you have done so?

　— _____

3. Does the system know what you like? — _____

4. Does the system suggest what you should buy? — _____

Paragraph❹

主題文： _____

_____

📝 次の英語のキーワードすべてをヒントとして使って、人間のスタッフを再導入する店が有利になるかもしれないと筆者が考えている理由を日本語でまとめましょう。

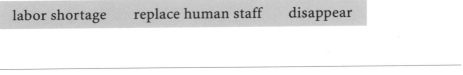

labor shortage　　replace human staff　　disappear

_____

_____

✔ **Grammar Check**　名詞の後に＜主語＋動詞＞が続く場合の解釈

I read the book last week. は 1 つの文ですが、語順を変えて the book I read last week とするとどうでしょうか。この場合、名詞（the book）の後に主語＋動詞（I read）がきて、それが前の名詞を修飾し、「私が先週読んだ本」という意味になります。元の文では the book は動詞 read の目的語だったので、book と I の間には目的格の関係代名詞（この場合は which もしくは that）が省略されていると解釈することができます。

📝 次の英文は Analysis 本文からの抜粋です。下線部に注意して、訳を完成させしましょう。

After entering, customers simply put <u>the items they want</u> into their shopping bags.

訳：入った後、客は単に（　　　　　　　　　　　　　　　　　　　　　）だけだ。

Report Completion

巻末 p. 116 にある **Report 8** の **Ⅲ** ~ **Ⅴ** に答えましょう。

Interview in Future Japan

🔊 25

イレブンマートの前で買い物客がインタビューを受けています。その音声を聴き、次の英文がインタビューの内容に合っていれば True に、合っていなければ False に ✓ を入れましょう。

1. The customer is a resident in the town. ☐ True ☐ False

2. The customer needs to be assisted in shopping. ☐ True ☐ False

3. The customer lives with her son's family. ☐ True ☐ False

Writing Composition

Analysis 本文中の [ ] 内の表現を使って、次の日本語の意味を表す英文を完成させましょう。

1. このロボットとの触れ合いは人との触れ合いに類似している。[similar to]

The (   ) (   ) this robot (   )
(   ) (   ) that with a person.

2. この店には客を認識するセンサーが備え付けられている。[equipped with]

This store (   ) (   ) (   ) (   )
that (   ) customers.

3. 私は考えを変えて、大きいほうのバッグを買った。[change *one's* mind]

I (   ) (   ) (   ) (   )
(   ) the bigger bag.

4. この店に入るにはスマートフォンが必要だ。[so that S + V]

(   ) (   ) your smartphone (   )
(   ) (   ) can (   ) (   )
(   ).

5. 当分の間、あなたの銀行口座から支払い金は引き落とせません。[for the time being]

(   ) cannot be deducted from your (   ) (   )
(   ) (   ) (   ) (   ).

Japanese are first humans to set foot on Mars

Japanese <u>astronauts</u> became the first humans to step on the <u>surface</u> of Mars earlier today. In a message that took eight minutes to arrive on Earth, mission leader Kei Onishi's first words were, "For all of <u>mankind</u>, I take this first step into the <u>galaxy</u>." Minutes later, Onishi was joined on the surface by fellow astronaut, Shizuka Taguchi. As the first humans to step on Mars, the Japanese Mars Team (JMT) have won the $1 billion <u>prize</u> in the international competition announced in 2032 by the <u>billionaire</u> owner of a software company. JMT has <u>narrowly</u> <u>defeated</u> an American team that is <u>due to</u> arrive next month. Onishi and his team of four Japanese astronauts plan to spend 18 months conducting <u>experiments</u> on the Martian surface before heading back to Earth in 2042.

 この記事のヘッドラインを日本語にしましょう。

Vocabulary Check

次の意味に該当するものを記事中の下線を引いた単語または語句から抜き出しましょう。ただし、動詞は原形で答えましょう。

1. かろうじて _____
2. 宇宙飛行士 _____
3. …する予定で _____
4. 実験 _____
5. 表面 _____
6. 億万長者 _____
7. …を打ち破る _____
8. 賞 _____
9. 人類 _____
10. 銀河 _____

Comprehension

空所に適語を記入して、記事の要旨を完成させましょう。

日本人の宇宙飛行士たちが、人類で初めて（　　　　　　　　　　　　　）ことにより、国際的なコンテストで（　　　　　　　　　　　　）を手にした。このコンテストは 2032 年に（　　　　　　　　　　　　　　　　　）が発表していたもので、日本のチームは（　　　　　　　　　　　）にわずかな差で勝った。

Report Completion

巻末 p. 117 にある **Report 9** の Ⅰ と Ⅱ に答えましょう。

Analysis

1   Mars is the second closest planet to Earth. The closest, Venus, is far too hot and   01
dangerous to even consider sending a human to. While Mars is very cold and ① <u>more</u>   02
<u>distant</u>, it presents a ② <u>realistic opportunity</u> to allow humans to survive there.   03

2   However, going to Mars is a big challenge for several reasons. It is far away so it   04
would take about nine months in a spacecraft to get there. Once there, astronauts would   05
have to stay for about a year and half before the Earth and Mars get close enough   06
together in space to make the return trip in about nine months. This means a total of   07
about three years for several humans to ③ <u>be confined</u> in a small space together. Thus, it   08
would be ④ <u>a huge psychological challenge</u> for the crew to get along with each other.   09

3   Then there are the technical challenges. Enough food and water has to be carried to   10
last for close to three years. This means the ⑤ <u>liquid</u> from human waste needs to be   11
recycled. Also, because ⑥ <u>the Martian atmosphere</u> is so thin, enough oxygen needs to be   12
carried along. There is also the challenge of protecting the astronauts from ⑦ <u>harmful</u>   13
<u>radiation</u>. All of these challenges will require new technologies and, of course, a lot of   14
money, to overcome. The huge cost may be too great for ⑧ <u>government supported</u>   15
<u>organizations</u> such as NASA, so sponsorship may come from billionaires.   16

4   These are just a few of the many problems that must be solved before a successful   17
mission is undertaken. However, imagine when ⑨ <u>our ancient ancestors</u>, such as the   18
Polynesians, first saw an island on the horizon across the sea. It must have seemed   19
impossibly out of reach. Through teamwork and ⑩ <u>technical intelligence</u> though, they   20
managed to build a boat and reached that island. Surely we will eventually do the same   21
with Mars.   22

NOTES   Venus「金星」 allow ～ to *do*「～に・・・（することを可能に）させる」
get along with ...「…と仲良くやっていく」 human waste「人間の排泄物」
out of reach「手が届かない」 manage to *do*「なんとか…する」

Vocabulary Check

空所に適語を記入して、Analysis 本文中の下線を引いた単語や語句の意味を完成させましょう。

① もっと（　　　　　）   ④ 大きな（　　　　　　）課題

② （　　　　　　）好機   ⑤ （　　　　　　　　）

③ （　　　　　　　）   ⑥ 火星の（　　　　　　）

⑦ （　　　　　　　） 放射線　　　　　⑨ 私たちの大昔の （　　　　　　）

⑧ 政府に支援された （　　　　　）　　⑩ 技術的な （　　　　）

Comprehension

Analysis 本文の各パラグラフにおいて、その主題文（1〜2文）を抜き出しましょう。その後、各パラグラフに関する設問に答えましょう。

Paragraph❶

主題文：＿＿＿＿＿＿＿＿＿＿＿＿＿＿＿＿＿＿＿＿＿＿＿＿＿＿＿

＿＿＿＿＿＿＿＿＿＿＿＿＿＿＿＿＿＿＿＿＿＿＿＿＿＿＿＿＿＿＿＿

✎ 空所に適語を記入して、金星ではなくて火星が探査の対象となる理由を完成させましょう。

金星は火星より （　　　　　　　　　　　） が、（　　　　　　　　　　　　　） である。

Paragraph❷

主題文：＿＿＿＿＿＿＿＿＿＿＿＿＿＿＿＿＿＿＿＿＿＿＿＿＿＿＿

(A) 空所に適する語句や数字を記入して、本文で述べられている情報を整理しましょう。

（　　　）から（　　　）までの往路	約（　　）か月
（　　　）での滞在期間	約（　　）年（　　）か月
（　　　）から（　　　）までの復路	約（　　）か月
合計	約（　　）年

(B) 往復に要する期間の長さから生じる課題を日本語で答えましょう。

＿＿＿＿＿＿＿＿＿＿＿＿＿＿＿＿＿＿＿＿＿＿＿＿＿＿＿＿＿＿＿＿

＿＿＿＿＿＿＿＿＿＿＿＿＿＿＿＿＿＿＿＿＿＿＿＿＿＿＿＿＿＿＿＿

Paragraph❸

主題文：_____

📝 次の英文は技術上の課題について述べたものです。空所に適語を記入しましょう。

1. They need to carry enough _____ to last for about three years.

2. They need to _____ from human waste.

3. They need to carry enough oxygen because the _____ .

4. Astronauts must be protected from _____ .

Paragraph❹

主題文：_____
_____

📝 次の英語のキーワードすべてをヒントとして使って、第 4 パラグラフの最終文にある the same
が指す内容を日本語でまとめましょう。

| the Polynesians | an island | out of reach | teamwork | technical intelligence |

_____
_____

✅ **Grammar Check**　断定を避けるために用いられる助動詞

She is very busy. は「彼女はとても忙しい」ということを事実として断定しています。では、
断定した言い方を避けたいときはどうすればよいでしょうか。1 つの方法は助動詞（must、
should、will、may、can）を用いることです。例えば must を使って She must be very
busy. とすると、「彼女はとても忙しいに違いない」という意味になります。なお、助動詞の過去
形（would、might、could）を用いると、さらに断定の度合いが弱くなります。

📝 次の英文は Analysis 本文からの抜粋です。下線部に注意して、訳を完成させしましょう。

Once there, astronauts <u>would have to stay</u> for about a year and half before the
Earth and Mars get close enough together in space to make the return trip in
about nine months.

訳：いったんそこに着いたなら、宇宙飛行士は（　　　　　　　　　　　　　　　　）を行うの
　　に十分なだけ地球と火星が近づくまで、（　　　　　　　　　　　　　　　　　　　　　）。

● Report Completion

巻末 p. 118 にある **Report 9** の **Ⅲ** ～ **Ⅴ** に答えましょう。

🖊 Interview in Future Japan　　　　　　　　🔊 28

宇宙工学を専攻する学生がインタビューを受けています。その音声を聴き、次の英文がインタビューの内容に合っていれば True に、合っていなければ False に ✓ を入れましょう。

1. The student was born before the Mars project started.　　　　□ True □ False

2. The Hayabusa project inspired the student.　　　　□ True □ False

3. The student believes the achievement of the project will be useful 　□ True □ False
for future projects.

● Writing Composition

記事中または Analysis 本文中の ［　　］内の表現を使って、次の日本語の意味を表す英文を完成させましょう。

1. その日本の宇宙船は来月、月面に到着する予定だ。［due to］

The Japanese spacecraft (　　　　　　　) (　　　　　　　) (　　　　　　　)
(　　　　　　　) on the (　　　　　　　) of the moon next month.

2. 彼らはチームワークのおかげでそのプロジェクトに成功することができた。［allow ～ to *do*］

Their (　　　　　　　) (　　　　　　　) (　　　　　　　) (　　　　　　　)
(　　　　　　　) in the project.

3. 国際宇宙ステーションでは異なる国の人々が互いに仲良くやっている。［get along with］

At International Space Station, people (　　　　　　　) (　　　　　　　)
(　　　　　　　) are (　　　　　　　) (　　　　　　　) (　　　　　　　)
one another.

4. 宇宙旅行は手が届かないものと私たちのほとんどが思っている。［out of reach］

(　　　　　) (　　　　　　　) (　　　　　　　) think that space travel
(　　　　　) (　　　　　　　) (　　　　　　　) (　　　　　　　).

5. アポロ 13 号の乗組員は多くの困難の後、どうにか生還した。［manage to *do*］

The crew of Apollo 13 (　　　　　　　) (　　　　　　　) (　　　　　　　) alive
(　　　　　　　) many (　　　　　　　).

29

Japan joins NPTO

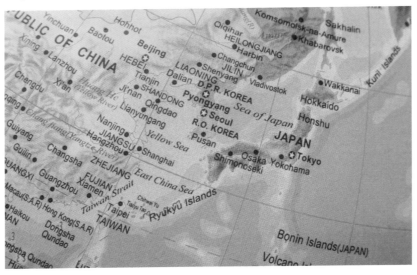

Today Japan became an official member of the North Pacific Trade Organization (NPTO) joining Korea and China to <u>form</u> the most powerful trading <u>block</u> of countries in the world. Prime Minister Sachiko Suzuki called today's <u>move</u> a "win-win-win situation." In 2035, China, and the newly <u>merged</u> "Korea," joining the North and South, invited Japan to join NPTO, and discussions began. Suzuki commented that the five years of <u>bargaining</u> with China and Korea were very challenging, but a <u>breakthrough</u> was reached last month. The next big challenge will be to form a common <u>currency</u> for the three countries, much like the Euro in Europe. The <u>target</u> year for the new common currency, called the "yon," will be 2045. Suzuki claimed that developing the yon, which is an invented <u>term</u> combining the yen, the yuan (China) and the won (Korea), should be easy. "Nobody uses cash these days, so changing to the yon will <u>pose</u> fewer problems," said Suzuki.

 この記事のヘッドラインを日本語にしましょう。

Vocabulary Check

次の意味に該当するものを記事中の下線を引いた単語から抜き出しましょう。ただし、動詞は原形で答えましょう。

1. 目標 _____

2. …を作り上げる _____

3. まとまり _____

4. 交渉する _____

5. 用語 _____

6. 手立て _____

7. …を併合する _____

8. …を引き起こす _____

9. 通貨 _____

10.打開 _____

Comprehension

空所に適語を記入して、記事の要旨を完成させましょう。

日本が（　　　　　　　　　　　　　　　　）になり、朝鮮と中国と共に形成する（　　　　　　　　）が誕生した。2035 年に（　　　　　　）が始まり、（　　　　　　　）の末、ついに先月合意に達した。（　　　　　　　　　　　　　）については2045 年の導入を目指している。

Report Completion

巻末 p. 119 にある **Report 10** の **I** と **II** に答えましょう。

Analysis

30

1   Globalization is gradually bringing countries closer together. Trading blocks of countries, such as the European Union (EU) or ASEAN, ① <u>have existed</u> for many years and have brought great benefits to people living there. The lack of tariffs among countries forming ② <u>a free trade agreement</u> means prices for goods from each other's nations are lower. It is also easier to travel, work and live in countries within the same block. Even travelers from countries outside of a block can benefit. ③ <u>Presently</u>, if you travel to EU countries, you can use the Euro everywhere, and after arrival, there is no need to go through the customs of each member country. Thus, trade agreements bring great advantages.

2   China and Japan have the second and third largest economies in the world respectively. As expected, there is ④ <u>a huge amount of trade</u> between the two countries. Japanese products, such as cars and electronics are very popular in China, and low-cost Chinese products are everywhere in Japan. ⑤ <u>Easily-attained</u> travel visas between the two countries have created ⑥ <u>a tourism boom</u>.

3   However, there is less trade between Japan and South Korea than one would expect for two countries that are so ⑦ <u>close geographically</u>. For example, cars from the world's fourth biggest ⑧ <u>automobile manufacturer</u>, Hyundai/Kia, are seldom seen in Japan. And cars from Toyota, the world's biggest maker, are not so common in South Korea. And between Japan and North Korea, there is virtually no trade.

4   Although it may seem farfetched that North and South Korea would become one country, the same was said about East and West Germany in the 1980s. Furthermore, in the middle of the 20th century, no one could imagine ⑨ <u>enemies</u> like France and Germany would ever share the same currency and open borders. While the NPTO may seem very unlikely ⑩ <u>at the moment</u>, enemies can sometimes become friends overnight. Friendships between countries can change very quickly, especially when the member countries can see some economic advantages.

NOTES   bring ... together「…を団結させる」 tariff「関税」 respectively「(述べられた順に)それぞれ」 Hyundai/Kia「ヒュンダイーキア[現代ー起亜]」(韓国の国内 1、2 位の自動車メーカーが形成する自動車企業グループ。起亜は現代の傘下) virtually「事実上」 farfetched「信じがたい」 furthermore「さらに」 overnight「一夜にして、突然に」

Vocabulary Check

空所に適語を記入して、Analysis 本文中の下線を引いた単語または語句の意味を完成させましょう。

① (　　　　　　　　) きた

② 自由貿易の (　　　　　　)

③ (　　　　　　　)

④ (　　　　　　　　　　) 貿易

⑤ 簡単に (　　　　　　　　　)

⑥ (　　　　　　　　　) のブーム

⑦ (　　　　　　　　) 近い

⑧ (　　　　　　　　) のメーカー

⑨ (　　　　　　)

⑩ (　　　　　　)

Comprehension

Analysis 本文の各パラグラフにおいて、その主題文（1〜2文）を抜き出しましょう。その後、各パラグラフに関する設問に答えましょう。

Paragraph❶

主題文：＿＿＿＿＿＿＿＿＿＿＿＿＿＿＿＿＿＿＿＿＿＿＿＿＿＿＿＿

📝 以下の書き出しに続けて、1つの貿易圏としての統合がもたらす利点をまとめましょう。

1. 関税がないので ＿＿＿＿＿＿＿＿＿＿＿＿＿＿＿＿＿＿＿＿＿。

2. 同じ圏内では ＿＿＿＿＿＿＿＿＿＿＿＿＿＿＿＿＿＿＿＿＿。

3. 圏外の国からの旅行者も ＿＿＿＿＿＿＿＿＿＿＿＿＿＿＿＿＿。

Paragraph❷

主題文：＿＿＿＿＿＿＿＿＿＿＿＿＿＿＿＿＿＿＿＿＿＿＿＿＿＿＿＿

📝 次の英文の内容が本文に合うように、空所に適する単語を記入しましょう。

1. The largest economy in the world is the U.S.A., and the second is (　　　　　).

2. China buys a lot of (　　　　　) (　　　　　), and they sell a lot of theirs to Japan.

3. It is easy to get (　　　　　) (　　　　　) to move between Japan and China, so a lot of travelers can come and go.

Paragraph❸

主題文： _____

_____

📝　以下は、日本と韓国の貿易について述べたものです。空所に適語を記入しましょう。

両国の貿易は（　　　　　　　　　　　　　　　　　　　　　　　　）。

例：韓国のヒュンダイ－キアの車は（　　　　　　　　　　　　　　）し、トヨタの車は

　　（　　　　　　　　　　　　　　）。

Paragraph❹

主題文： _____

_____

(A) 第4パラグラフ内で、24行目にある enemies can sometimes become friends overnight
　　の具体的事例として挙げられているものを2つ、日本語で答えましょう。

・ _____　　・ _____

(B) 次の質問に英語で答えましょう。

According to the author, what do two countries that used to be enemies need to see to

form friendly relations? — _____

✓ **Grammar Check**	頻度を表す副詞

頻度を表す副詞を程度の順に並べると、次のようになります。

　　always > usually > often > sometimes > seldom > rarely > hardly > never

always の頻度は 100 パーセント、never は 0 パーセントです。いずれの語も、英文内で置かれる
基本的な位置は be 動詞の後や一般動詞の前であり、助動詞が入る場合には助動詞の後となります。

📝　次の英文は Analysis 本文からの抜粋です。下線部に注意して、訳を完成させしましょう。

For example, cars from the world's fourth biggest automobile manufacturer,
Hyundai/Kia, are <u>seldom</u> seen in Japan.

訳：例えば、（　　　　　　　　　　　　　　　　　　　　　　　　）は、

　　日本では（　　　　　　　　　　　　　　　）。

● Report Completion

巻末 p. 120 にある **Report 10** の **Ⅲ** ～ **Ⅴ** に答えましょう。

✎ Interview in Future Japan　🔊 31

関西国際空港に到着した韓国人旅行者がインタビューを受けています。その音声を聴き、次の英文が
インタビューの内容に合っていれば True に、合っていなければ False に ✓ を入れましょう。

1. The Korean has already heard about the news that Japan would　☐ True ☐ False
join NPTO.

2. The Korean often comes to Japan to eat Japanese foods.　☐ True ☐ False

3. The Korean wouldn't need to come to Japan to buy things.　☐ True ☐ False

Writing Composition

Analysis 本文中の ［　　］内の表現を使って、次の日本語の意味を表す英文を完成させましょう。

1. EU は 1993 年にヨーロッパの国々を政治的、経済的に 1 つにするために始まった。

［bring ... together］

The EU (　　　　　　) (　　　　　　　　) 1993 to (　　　　　　) (　　　　　　　)

(　　　　　　) (　　　　　　　　) politically and economically.

2. 円、元、ウォンはそれぞれ、日本、中国、韓国の通貨である。［respectively］

The yen, the yuan and the won are (　　　　　　) (　　　　　　) (　　　　　　),

(　　　　　　) and (　　　　　　) (　　　　　　) (　　　　　　).

3. 毎年、日本は大量の食糧を海外から輸入している。［a huge amount of］

Every year, Japan imports (　　　　　　) (　　　　　　) (　　　　　　)

(　　　　　　) (　　　　　　) (　　　　　　) overseas.

4. この店では日本製の商品はほとんど売られていない。［seldom］

Products (　　　　　　) (　　　　　　) (　　　　　　) (　　　　　　)

(　　　　　　) (　　　　　　) at this store.

5. ドイツを 2 つの国に分断していたベルリンの壁は一夜にして壊された。［overnight］

The Berlin Wall, (　　　　　　) had split Germany (　　　　　　) two

countries, (　　　　　　) torn down (　　　　　　).

32

Japan's population no longer declining

The great <u>decline</u> in Japan's population predicted just a couple of decades ago has failed to happen. The <u>statistics</u> just released by the government <u>reveal</u> that Japan's population grew <u>slightly</u> for the first time in 30 years. The population now in 2040 is slightly more than 115 million and is <u>projected</u> to <u>reach</u> 130 million people by 2060. By that year, Japan's population will be growing by over one million people a year. This dramatic <u>reversal</u> in the <u>downward</u> trend arrives at the same time that the new average <u>lifespan</u> for women has reached 100 years and men can expect to live for 94 years. Population forecaster, Yuta Kitayama, said, "We did not anticipate the big <u>medical</u> advances that have helped people live longer."

 この記事のヘッドラインを日本語にしましょう。

Vocabulary Check

次の意味に該当するものを記事中の下線を引いた単語から抜き出しましょう。ただし、動詞は原形で答えましょう。

1. 医学の _____
2. 寿命 _____
3. 統計 _____
4. 逆転 _____
5. …を予想する _____
6. 下方へ _____
7. わずかに _____
8. 減少 _____
9. …を明らかにする _____
10. …に達する _____

Comprehension

空所に適語を記入して、記事の要旨を完成させましょう。

政府発表の統計によると、日本の人口は（　　　　　　　　　　　　　　　　　）。
2040 年に（　　　　　　　　　　　　　　　）である人口は、2060 年までには
（　　　　　　　　　　　　　　　）と予想される。下降傾向は逆転したが、人口予測官のキタヤマユウタ氏は、（　　　　　　　　　　　　　　　　　　　）と話した。

Report Completion

巻末 p. 121 にある **Report 11** の **I** と **II** に答えましょう。

Analysis

33

1   Japan's population is ①dropping, and the rate of decline is increasing. There are two main reasons for the decline: the fertility rate is low (less than 1.5 babies per woman), and Japan does not welcome many ②immigrants. Although many developed countries have a similarly low fertility rate, they tend to allow immigration, which keeps their population either ③stable or growing. ④Population forecasts show that Japan will have only 83 million people at the end of this century, and if the trend continues, the population could decline to zero by the year 3000! However, changes that help people live longer, or to have more children, or to allow more people to immigrate to Japan are all possible.

2   Two ⑤leading causes of death in Japan, cancer and heart disease, are ailments for which medical science is rapidly finding ⑥cures. For cancer, gene therapy is just one of a few new approaches that stop tumors from growing, or even make them disappear. For heart disease, new surgical techniques combined with new drugs are turning it into a chronic disease, rather than a ⑦deadly one. Similarly, new drugs for hepatitis and diabetes, two other big killers in Japan, are already ⑧lengthening lives. All of these advances in medicine could help people live significantly longer lives, reducing the death rate.

3   At the other end of life, improvements in techniques for ⑨eliminating genetic diseases among babies and also for improving fertility among couples are advancing quickly. Older couples may routinely be bearing healthy children in the near future as the fertile period lengthens.

4   Finally, ⑩conservative views about immigration could quickly change. It is the younger generation who will be making the laws in the future, and they are more open to immigration. Allowing more foreigners to immigrate could quickly raise Japan's population.

5   Although all of the developments mentioned here may not halt Japan's population decline, they show that the predicted drop in population is far from certain.

NOTES   fertility rate「出生率」 tend to *do*「…する傾向がある」 ailment「病気」 gene therapy「遺伝子治療」
stop ... from *doing*「…に〜させない」 tumor「腫瘍」 surgical technique「外科的技術」
turn A into B「A を B に変える」 chronic disease「慢性病」 hepatitis「肝炎」
diabetes「糖尿病」 routinely「普通に」 fertile period「妊娠可能期間」
far from ...「…からは程遠い」

Vocabulary Check

空所に適語を記入して、Analysis 本文中の下線を引いた単語や語句の意味を完成させましょう。

① (　　　　　　　　　　)　　　　⑥ (　　　　　　　　　　　)
② (　　　　　　　　　　)　　　　⑦ (　　　　　　　　　　　)
③ (　　　　　　　　　　)　　　　⑧ 寿命を (　　　　　　　　　　)
④ 人口の (　　　　　　)　　　　⑨ 遺伝子的な病気を (　　　　　　　　　　)
⑤ (　　　　　　) 原因　　　　⑩ (　　　　　　　　) 見方

Comprehension

Analysis 本文の各パラグラフにおいて、その主題文（1～2文）を抜き出しましょう。その後、各パラグラフに関する設問に答えましょう。

Paragraph❶

主題文：_____

(A) 筆者が挙げている日本の人口減少の主な原因を2つ、日本語で答えましょう。

・_____　・_____

(B) 本文で示されている次の数値は、それぞれ何を表しているでしょうか。日本語で答えましょう。

less than 1.5	
83 million	
zero	

Paragraph❷

主題文：_____

_____

次の質問に英語で答えましょう。

1. What could make tumors smaller or even disappear? — _____

2. What could stop people with heart disease from dying?

— _____

Paragraph❸

主題文：_____

_____

🖉 次の英文の内容が本文に合うように、空所に適する単語を記入しましょう。

Thanks to (　　　　　) (　　　　　) (　　　　　　　), it may be possible to (　　　　　)
genetic diseases among babies and to (　　　　　) the fertile period of humans.

Paragraph❹

主題文：_____

🖉 空所に適語を記入して、移民が日本の人口増加につながる可能性についてまとめましょう。

将来、(　　　　　　　　　) 立場の若い世代は (　　　　　　　　　　　　　　　) ので、
より多くの外国人を移民させることによって日本の人口は急速に増えるかもしれない。

✓ Grammar Check　it is/was ... that/who ～の強調構文

My brother broke the radio.（私の弟がそのラジオを壊した）
上の文の the radio の部分を強調して「私の弟が壊したのはそのラジオだ」と言うときは、まず
It is the radio（そのラジオだ）と述べ、その後に that my brother broke と続けて次のように
します。

It is the radio that my brother broke.

では、「そのラジオを壊したのは私の弟だ」と言うときはどうしますか。my brother を強調した
いので、次のようになります。

It is my brother that broke the radio.

ただし、この文のように強調する対象が人物であり、その行為の主語となる場合は that だけでな
く who もよく使われます。

🖉 次の英文は Analysis 本文からの抜粋です。下線部に注意して、訳を完成させしましょう。

It is the younger generation who will be making the laws in the future, and they
are more open to immigrants.

訳：将来、(　　　　　　　　　　　　　　) で、彼らは (　　　　　　　　　　　　　)
　　である。

74

Report Completion

巻末 p. 122 にある **Report 11** の **Ⅲ** ～ **Ⅴ** に答えましょう。

Interview in Future Japan

🔊 34

人口予測官のキタヤマ氏がインタビューを受けています。その音声を聴き、次の英文がインタビューの内容に合っていれば True に、合っていなければ False に ✓ を入れましょう。

1. Kitayama expected that Japan's population would be under 100 million 20 years ago. ☐ True ☐ False

2. Kitayama says that the medical advances have improved Japanese lifespan. ☐ True ☐ False

3. Kitayama wants elderly people to work to help Japanese society. ☐ True ☐ False

Writing Composition

Analysis 本文中の [ ] 内の表現を使って、次の日本語の意味を表す英文を完成させましょう。

1. 女性は男性より長生きする傾向がある。[tend to *do*]

(   ) (   ) (   ) (   ) longer
(   ) men.

2. 保守的な人々の中には、移民が自分の国に移り住むことを阻止したいと思っている人たちがいる。[stop ... from *doing*]

Some (   ) people want to (   ) (   )
(   ) (   ) into their country.

3. 医療の進歩が高齢者を労働力の重要な一部に変えた。[turn A into B]

(   ) (   ) have (   ) (   )
(   ) (   ) an important part of the labor force.

4. 世界には安定からは程遠い国がたくさんある。[far from]

In the world, (   ) (   ) a lot of countries that are
(   ) (   ) stable.

5. その国の人口を支えているのは南米からの移民たちだ。[it is ... that ～]

It is (   ) (   ) (   ) (   )
(   ) maintain the country's population.

Japan's two biggest brewers merge

Japan's two biggest beer companies, Rikin and Azahi, announced an agreement to merge <u>operations</u> starting next year. The announcement came on the news that beer <u>consumption</u> hit another low last year. Japanese now drink only about one half the amount of beer <u>per capita</u> that they drank at the peak in 1992. "People are simply drinking less and less of all alcoholic <u>beverages</u>," <u>claimed</u> Hideki Ogawa, CEO of Azahi. "We had no <u>choice</u> but to join up with Rikin because sales kept going down <u>year after year</u>. Millennials and Gen Z seem to drink beer only on special <u>occasions</u>. Even on hot days, they <u>prefer</u> sparkling water to beer. And the baby boomers who <u>used to</u> drink a lot of beer are either drinking less for health reasons or dying off."

NOTES millennials「ミレニアル世代」（1980年代から2000年代初頭に生まれた世代）
Gen Z「Z世代」（1990年代半ばから2000年代前半に生まれた世代。Gen は Generation の略）

 この記事のヘッドラインを日本語にしましょう。

Vocabulary Check

次の意味に該当するものを記事中の下線を引いた単語または語句から抜き出しましょう。ただし、動詞は原形で答えましょう。

1. 行事 _____
2. 年々 _____
3. 事業 _____
4. かつてはよく…した _____
5. 消費 _____
6. 選択肢 _____
7. 飲料 _____
8. …を主張する _____
9. …のほうを好む _____
10. 1 人当たり _____

Comprehension

空所に適語を記入して、記事の要旨を完成させましょう。

昨年、ビールの消費量が（　　　　　　　　　　　　　　　）し、日本の 2 大ビール会社のリキンとアザヒは（　　　　　　　　　　　　　　　）と発表した。ビールの 1 人当たりの消費量は（　　　　　　　　　）に比べて（　　　　　　　　　　　　　　　）で、アザヒのオガワヒデキ CEO は「（　　　　　　　　　　　　　　）がだんだん飲まれなくなっていて、年々（　　　　　　　）ため、リキンとの合併以外に選択肢はなかった」と語った。

Report Completion

巻末 p. 123 にある **Report 12** の **I** と **II** に答えましょう。

Analysis

1   Alcohol, in its many forms, such as beer, sake, wine and whiskey, has been playing ①an important role in ②Japanese socializing, but this seems to be changing. Much of this socializing occurs in the evenings after work. However, attitudes towards the work-family balance are changing. Evening drinking sessions where all company staff go to an *izakaya* to drink are ③gradually declining. Young employees are feeling more power to ④resist their bosses when invited to go drinking after work. They don't want to be like their fathers who came home late most nights. Instead, they would rather spend their evenings with their spouses and children.

2   This change is also related to gender roles and the growing ⑤equality between men and women in society. Now, wives expect their husbands to be more involved in family life including raising their children. Likewise, women employees are resisting the after-work drinking sessions where they would just ⑥pour beer and ⑦pretend to laugh at their boss's jokes.

3   The risks involved in drinking alcohol are also more ⑧widely publicized now. It is not only the damage, such as liver disease and cancer, that alcohol can do to the human body. Accidents, such as when people are killed or injured by drunk drivers, or when a university student dies from ⑨alcohol poisoning after a chugging contest, ⑩warn people about the dangers of drinking too much.

4   Then there are the changing tastes of consumers to consider. For example, sake consumption is now just one-third of what it was in the 1970s, although overseas sales of sake are booming. Young people are now more exposed to a world of alcoholic beverages through travel and social media than their parents were. However, perhaps one big reason for changing tastes is the price. Young people may prefer *chuhai* because it gets them feeling good for a lower price than beer.

NOTES   would rather ... 「むしろ…したい」 spouse 「配偶者」 gender role 「性差による役割」
be involved in ... 「…に関わる」 likewise 「その上」 liver disease 「肝臓病」
cancer 「がん」 chugging contest 「一気飲み」 be exposed to ... 「…に接する」

Vocabulary Check

空所に適語を記入して、Analysis 本文中の下線を引いた単語や語句の意味を完成させましょう。

① 重要な（　　　　　　　）　　　　⑥ ビールを（　　　　　　　）

② 日本人の（　　　　　　）　　　　⑦ 笑う（　　　　　　　　）

③ （　　　　　　　）減っている　　⑧ 広く（　　　　　　　　）

④ 上司に（　　　　　　）　　　　　⑨ アルコール（　　　　　　）

⑤ （　　　　　　）　　　　　　　　⑩ 人々に（　　　　　　　）

Comprehension

Analysis 本文の各パラグラフにおいて、その主題文（1～2文）を抜き出しましょう。その後、各パラグラフに関する設問に答えましょう。

Paragraph❶

主題文：＿＿＿＿＿＿＿＿＿＿＿＿＿＿＿＿＿＿＿＿＿＿＿＿＿＿＿＿＿＿＿＿

＿＿＿＿＿＿＿＿＿＿＿＿＿＿＿＿＿＿＿＿＿＿＿＿＿＿＿＿＿＿＿＿＿＿＿

空所に適語を記入して、日本人のアルコールに対する意識の変化をまとめましょう。

これまで	アルコールは（　　　　　　　　　　　　　）を果たし、そうした社交のほとんどは（　　　　　　　　　　　　）で行われた。
昨今	若い社員は上司に（　　　　　　　　　）、夜は（　　　　　　　）を好む。

Paragraph❷

主題文：＿＿＿＿＿＿＿＿＿＿＿＿＿＿＿＿＿＿＿＿＿＿＿＿＿＿＿＿＿＿＿＿

＿＿＿＿＿＿＿＿＿＿＿＿＿＿＿＿＿＿＿＿＿＿＿＿＿＿＿＿＿＿＿＿＿＿＿

次の英文の内容が本文に合うように、空所に適する単語を記入しましょう。

1. Wives want (　　　　　) (　　　　　　) to do housework for their family.
2. Women employees don't want to (　　　　　) (　　　　　) and pretend to
   (　　　　) at after-work drinking sessions.

Paragraph❸

主題文：_____

✎ 次のキーワードに関わる飲酒のリスクの内容を、それぞれ日本語で答えましょう。

health: _____

accident: _____

Paragraph❹

主題文：_____

✎ 次の質問に英語で答えましょう。

1. Today, is sake consumption less than half of that in the 1970s? — _____

2. Do young Japanese get more information on alcoholic beverages through travel and social media than their parents? — _____

3. Is the price of alcohol likely to have something to do with young people's choices?

   — _____

✓ **Grammar Check**　接続詞の後の主語と be 動詞

when、if、while などの接続詞は、文と文をつなぐ働きをします。それぞれの接続詞の後には主語と述語となる動詞を含む文（以下、「接続詞が導く節」）が続きますが、接続詞が導く節内の主語が主節の主語と同じだったり、接続詞が導く節内の主語と be 動詞が明らかであったりする場合、そうした主語や be 動詞が省略されることがよくあります。

While *I was* staying in Japan, I visited Kyoto.

例えば、上の文なら I was を省略して次のようになります。

While staying in Japan, I visited Kyoto.

✎ 次の英文は Analysis 本文からの抜粋です。下線部に注意して、訳を完成させしましょう。

Young employees are feeling more power to resist their bosses <u>when invited</u> to go drinking after work.

訳：若い社員は（　　　　　　　　　　　　　　　　　）、上司に逆らう気持ちがより強くなっている。

Report Completion

巻末 p. 124 にある **Report 12** の **Ⅲ** ～ **Ⅴ** に答えましょう。

Interview in Future Japan

🔊 37

アザヒのオガワヒデキ氏がインタビューを受けています。その音声を聴き、次の英文がインタビューの内容に合っていれば True に、合っていなければ False に ✓を入れましょう

1. The two companies have decided the merger suddenly. □ True □ False

2. The two companies need to streamline their management. □ True □ False

3. Ogawa mentions another beer company which will stop beer production. □ True □ False

Writing Composition

記事中または Analysis 本文中の [   ] 内の表現を使って、次の日本語の意味を表す英文を完成させましょう。

1. 近隣の酒屋の数が年々減っている。[year after year]

(   ) (   ) of liquor stores in our (   ) has
been (   ) (   ) (   ) (   ).

2. 私が子どもの頃、父は私たちが寝た後、家に帰ってきたものだ。[used to]

(   ) I was a child, my father (   ) (   )
(   ) home after we (   ) (   )
(   ).

3. 外食するよりむしろピザを注文したい。[would rather]

I (   ) (   ) (   ) a pizza than
(   ) (   ).

4. その会社は長年日本酒の輸出に関わっている。[be involved in]

The company (   ) (   ) (   )
(   ) the (   ) of Japanese sake for years.

5. 若い世代は自分の親よりももっと外国文化に接している。[be exposed to]

The younger generation (   ) (   ) (   )
foreign cultures (   ) (   ) their parents.

38

Government introduces radical new university curriculum

The <u>long-awaited</u> new curriculum for university students will begin in September 2041, the Ministry of Education <u>announced</u> today. Although many of the changes had already been <u>leaked</u> over the past few months, the news still came as a shock to students and professors. Two of the biggest changes include starting the school year in September <u>instead of</u> April and using English as the language of <u>instruction</u> in <u>at least</u> half of all courses. Another big change is the requirement that a <u>minimum</u> of one half of all courses be held in virtual mode. These courses will be taught by <u>award-winning</u> professors by video from around the world and <u>purchased</u> by universities. Ministry spokesperson, Madoka Takemoto, claimed that the changes will help make Japanese students more <u>competitive</u> with students around the world.

 この記事のヘッドラインを日本語にしましょう。

Vocabulary Check

次の意味に該当するものを記事中の下線を引いた単語または語句から抜き出しましょう。ただし、動詞は原形で答えましょう。

1. …の代わりに _____
2. 受賞した _____
3. …を漏らす _____
4. 最低 _____
5. …を発表する _____
6. 少なくとも _____
7. 指導 _____
8. 長く待ち望まれていた _____
9. 競争力のある _____
10. …を購入する _____

Comprehension

空所に適語を記入して、記事の要旨を完成させましょう。

> 文部省は2041年9月から大学の新しいカリキュラムを導入すると発表。大きな変更点は、
> (　　　　　　　　　　　　　　　　　　　　　　　) こと、(
> 　　　　　　　　　　　) こと、(
> 　　　　　　　　　　　　　　　　　　　) ことの3点である。

Report Completion

巻末 p. 125 にある **Report 13** の Ⅰ と Ⅱ に答えましょう。

Analysis

39

1 Education at all levels is ① <u>undergoing dramatic changes</u> in several ways. Just two decades ago, there were very few international students studying at Japanese universities. Presently, the number is growing by over 10 percent every year. This increase is necessary to help many Japanese universities survive because the number of Japanese students is ② <u>declining rapidly</u>. However, foreign students tend to want to receive their education in English because they know it will give them maximum ③ <u>employment opportunities</u> after they graduate. For <u>this reason</u>, more courses are being offered in English in many countries where the native language is not English. If Japanese universities want to ④ <u>compete</u>, they will have to do likewise. And because in most of the world the school year begins in the autumn, Japanese universities may have to follow suit.

2 Massive Open Online Courses (MOOCs) are another development that could create ⑤ <u>a big disruption</u> in education. Presently, most MOOCs are offered for free over the Internet by hundreds of universities around the world; however, students generally cannot use them for credit. Some MOOCs are of very ⑥ <u>high quality</u> taught by famous instructors, which raises the question of whether these types of courses could replace our face-to-face courses taught at universities today. High-quality courses in virtual mode that students can watch on their own time may be sold as a package to universities in the future.

3 As noted in News 6, there may be a much greater focus on English listening and speaking skills. Students will need good English listening skills because many of their virtual classes will be ⑦ <u>conducted</u> in the world's lingua fránca. Instead of writing essays for their ⑧ <u>assignments</u>, students may submit in multimedia format such as making videos and designing websites. When they write essays, they will be able to ⑨ <u>compose in Japanese</u> and press a button to get a perfect translation into English. Just like spelling mistakes have ⑩ <u>become rare</u> with the spell checker, grammar and vocabulary mistakes will also disappear.

NOTES maximum「最大の」 do likewise「同様に行う」 follow suit「先例に倣う」
for free「無料で」 credit「履修単位」 whether S + V「S が V かどうか」
package「一括取引」 lingua fránca「国際語」

Vocabulary Check

空所に適語を記入して、Analysis 本文中の下線を引いた単語や語句の意味を完成させましょう。

① 劇的な変化を （　　　　　　　　　）　　　　⑥ 高い （　　　　　　）

② （　　　　　　　）減少している　　　　　　⑦ （　　　　　　）

③ （　　　　　　）の機会　　　　　　　　　　⑧ （　　　　　　）

④ （　　　　　　　　）　　　　　　　　　　　⑨ 日本語で （　　　　　　　　）

⑤ 大きな （　　　　　　　）　　　　　　　　⑩ （　　　　　　　　）なる

Comprehension

Analysis 本文の各パラグラフにおいて、その主題文（1〜2文）を抜き出しましょう。その後、各パラグラフに関する設問に答えましょう。

Paragraph❶

主題文：_____

(A) 日本が海外の大学の傾向に倣うべきだとしている点を2つ、日本語で答えましょう。

・_____

・_____

(B) 空所に適語を記入して、波下線で示した this reason についての説明を完成させましょう。

this reason とは、（　　　　　　　　　　　　　　　　　　　　　　　）
という問いに対する「理由」であり、その具体的な内容は「留学生が （

　　　　　　　　　　　　　　　　　　　）」というものである。

Paragraph❷

主題文：_____

_____

📝 MOOCs について、次の質問に英語で答えましょう。

1. Generally, what organizations offer MOOCs? — _____

2. Do we have to pay to use MOOCs? — _____

3. How can we access MOOCs? — _____

4. Can we take famous instructors' courses through MOOCs? — _____

主題文： _____

_____

📝 空所に適語を記入して、大学の授業の予想される未来図について整理しましょう。

1. (_____)

⇒ リスニングとスピーキングの技能を重視

2. 課題は論文を書かずに、（ _____ ）で提出。

3. 論文を書く場合は、（ _____ ）する。

⇒ 文法や語彙の間違いもなくなる。

✓ Grammar Check   受動態の進行形

The wall was painted white.

上の文の述部である was painted は＜be 動詞＋過去分詞＞の形の受動態で、文意は「その壁は白く塗られた」ですね。では、進行形の形で「その壁は白く塗られていた」とするにはどうしますか。

The wall was *being* painted white.

この文のように be 動詞の後に being を加えます。受動態の進行形では時制を問わず、being を be 動詞の後に入れます。

📝 次の英文は Analysis 本文からの抜粋です。下線部に注意して、訳を完成させしましょう。

For this reason, more courses <u>are being offered</u> in English in many countries where the native language is not English.

訳：この理由のために、（ _____ ）では、より多くの授業が

（ _____ ）。

● Report Completion

巻末 p. 126 にある **Report 13** の **Ⅲ** 〜 **Ⅴ** に答えましょう。

🖉 Interview in Future Japan　　　　🔊 40

ある日本の大学の近くで学生がインタビューを受けています。その音声を聴き、次の英文がインタビューの内容に合っていれば True に、合っていなければ False に ✓ を入れましょう

1. The student came to college to take classes.　　　　□ True □ False

2. The student is not satisfied with MOOCs.　　　　□ True □ False

3. The student wants to take classes face-to-face.　　　　□ True □ False

● Writing Composition

記事中または Analysis 本文中の［　　］内の表現を使って、次の日本語の意味を表す英文を完成させましょう。

1. 大学に行かないで、私はインターネットで授業を受けた。［instead of］

（　　　　　　　　）（　　　　　　　　　）（　　　　　　　　　）（　　　　　　　　　　）

（　　　　　　　　）, I took classes on the Internet.

2. 多くの国で、学年暦は 9 月に始まる。日本も同様にすべきだ。［do likewise］

In many countries, the school year（　　　　　　　　）（　　　　　　　　）

（　　　　　　　　）. Japan（　　　　　　　　）（　　　　　　　　）（　　　　　　　　）.

3. 兄はボストンで経営学を学び、私もそれに倣うことを決めた。［follow suit］

My brother studied（　　　　　　　　　　）in Boston, and I've（　　　　　　　　）

（　　　　　　）（　　　　　　　　）（　　　　　　　　）.

4. 無料でダウンロードできるウェブサイトには注意するべきだ。［for free］

We should（　　　　　　　　）（　　　　　　　　）（　　　　　　　　　）the websites that

we can（　　　　　　　　）（　　　　　　　　）（　　　　　　　　）.

5. 課題をインターネットで提出できるかどうか教えてくれますか。［whether S + V］

Could you tell me（　　　　　　　　）（　　　　　　　　）（　　　　　　　　）

（　　　　　　　　）the（　　　　　　　　）through the Internet?

41

Two die in first flying car accident

Two people were killed in Sendai yesterday when two flying cars collided in mid-air and fell to the ground. These were the first deaths recorded since urban private vehicle flight was allowed in Japan two years ago in 2049. The two cars were flying at a height of about 100 meters when they hit each other at a virtual intersection. Police are investigating the accident with some clues that suggest one of the cars was flying at the wrong height. Police Inspector Yuta Kurihara explained that cars going in an east-west direction must travel at a different height than those going north and south. Also, the automatic crash detection system must have failed. It appears that many of the safety mechanisms must have failed.

 この記事のヘッドラインを日本語にしましょう。

Vocabulary Check

次の意味に該当するものを記事中の下線を引いた単語から抜き出しましょう。ただし、動詞は原形で答えましょう。

1. …を調査する _____
2. 交差点 _____
3. 衝突する _____
4. 都市の _____
5. 方向 _____
6. 検知 _____
7. …を記録する _____
8. 高度 _____
9. 装置 _____
10. 手がかり _____

Comprehension

空所に適語を記入して、記事の要旨を完成させましょう。

仙台で（　　　　　　　　　　　　　　　　　　　）。これは 2049 年に（　　　　　　　　　　　
　　　　　　　） 以来、初めての死亡事故で、2 台は（　　　　　　　　　　） で衝突し、
どちらも高度（　　　　　　　　　　　　　　　　　　　）。警察の見解は、どちらかが（
　　　　　　　） ということで、さらには自動衝突検知システムが（　　　　　　　　　
　　　） 可能性が高いとしている。

Report Completion

巻末 p. 127 にある **Report 14** の Ⅰ と Ⅱ に答えましょう。

Analysis

42

1   Just over a century ago, the streets of Japanese cities were very different from our 01
modern ones. ①<u>A common sound</u> was the clop-clop of horses' hooves and a very 02
familiar ②<u>smell</u> was one of horse manure. Another common form of transport was the 03
rickshaw. Of course, this all changed at the beginning of the 20th century with 04
③<u>motorized vehicles</u>. Horses and rickshaws gradually disappeared from the streets of 05
urban Japan replaced by cars, trains and trams. 06

2   Now we may be reaching the limits of ④<u>surface vehicles</u>. ⑤<u>Enormous traffic jams</u> are 07
a feature of modern life. The famous U-turn during Japanese holidays sometimes leads 08
to jams that are dozens of kilometers long. Rather unbelievably, the traffic jams in 09
Japan's big cities are not as bad as those in cities overseas, such as Beijing and Manila. 10
⑥<u>Obviously</u>, flying vehicles have the potential to solve this problem, although the noise 11
and the wind they create will be a challenge to overcome. 12

3   Although ⑦<u>futuristic novels</u>, manga and anime sometimes describe flying cars, until 13
recently, they seemed like something that would only arrive in the distant future, if ever. 14
However, flying cars are becoming closer to reality. Already, some ⑧<u>prototypes</u> have 15
been built and tested. Some of these operate similar to a drone with several propellers 16
for vertical take-off and landing like a helicopter. Already, Dubai, which has terrible 17
traffic jams, is testing a flying taxi service. 18

4   Because it takes a lot of training to fly such machines, in the future, flying cars will 19
be completely automated. Passengers will simply enter their destination into the on- 20
board computer, which will understand ⑨<u>voice instructions</u>. Then, the self-flying car 21
will do the rest using artificial intelligence (AI). Because everything will be automated 22
using GPS and ⑩<u>collision avoidance</u>, accidents will be rare. 23

5   When our great grandchildren see images of today's surface vehicles, they may have 24
the same impression that we have now when we see pictures of rickshaws. 25

NOTES   clop-clop「(馬の蹄 [ひづめ] の) パッカパッカ (という音)」 hooves < hoof「蹄」
manure「馬や牛のふん」 rickshaw「人力車」 if ever「そうだとしても」
become closer to ...「…により近くなる」 on-board「搭載された」 the rest「残りのこと」

Vocabulary Check

空所に適語を記入して、Analysis 本文中の下線を引いた単語や語句の意味を完成させましょう。

① よくある（　　　　　　　）　　　　　　　　　② （　　　　　　　）

③（　　　　　　　　　　　　　　）乗り物　　　⑦（　　　　　　　）小説

④（　　　　　　　　）乗り物　　　　　⑧（　　　　　　　　）

⑤　ものすごい（　　　　　　　　）　　　⑨　声での（　　　　　　）

⑥（　　　　　　　）　　　　　　　　　⑩　衝突の（　　　　　　）

Comprehension

Analysis 本文の各パラグラフにおいて、その主題文（1〜2文）を抜き出しましょう。その後、各パラグラフに関する設問に答えましょう。

Paragraph❶

主題文：＿＿＿＿＿＿＿＿＿＿＿＿＿＿＿＿＿＿＿＿＿＿＿＿＿＿＿＿＿＿＿＿＿

＿＿＿＿＿＿＿＿＿＿＿＿＿＿＿＿＿＿＿＿＿＿＿＿＿＿＿＿＿＿＿＿＿＿＿＿＿

次の英文は、輸送手段の推移について述べたものです。空所に適する単語を記入しましょう。

More than a century ago, people used (　　　　　) and (　　　　　) as common forms
of transport. However, at the beginning of the 20th century, they started to use
(　　　　) (　　　　　) such as cars, trains and trams.

Paragraph❷

主題文：＿＿＿＿＿＿＿＿＿＿＿＿＿＿＿＿＿＿＿＿＿＿＿＿＿＿＿＿＿＿＿＿＿

筆者が陸上の乗り物は限界かもしれないと述べている理由を日本語で答えましょう。

＿＿＿＿＿＿＿＿＿＿＿＿＿＿＿＿＿＿＿＿＿＿＿＿＿＿＿＿＿＿＿＿＿＿＿＿＿

Paragraph❸

主題文：＿＿＿＿＿＿＿＿＿＿＿＿＿＿＿＿＿＿＿＿＿＿＿＿＿＿＿＿＿＿＿＿＿

書き出しに続けて、質問に対する答えを完成させましょう。

1. Why can we say that flying cars are becoming closer to reality?
   — Because some prototypes ＿＿＿＿＿＿＿＿＿＿＿＿＿＿＿＿＿＿＿＿＿＿.

2. How similar are some flying cars to drones?
   — Both of them have ＿＿＿＿＿＿＿＿＿＿＿＿＿＿＿＿＿＿＿＿＿＿＿＿.

Paragraph ❹

主題文：_____

 次の英語のキーワードすべてをヒントとして使って、完全自動の空飛ぶ車の操作方法について日本語でまとめましょう。

| passengers | destination | computer | artificial intelligence |

✔ Grammar Check　　as を使った比較表現の否定

I am **as** busy **as** you.

上の文は「私はあなたと同じくらい忙しい」と、忙しさの度合いが同程度であることを表します。否定文にすると次のようになります。

I am **not as** busy **as** you.（私はあなたほど忙しくない）

この文は、次のように比較級を使って言い換えることもできます。

You are bus**ier than** me.

また、冒頭の文を否定文にする場合、次のように最初の as を so にして比較のニュアンスを強調した表現にすることもできます。

I am **not so** busy **as** you.

 次の英文は Analysis 本文からの抜粋です。下線部に注意して、訳を完成させしましょう。

Rather unbelievably, the traffic jams in Japan's big cities are <u>not as bad as</u> those in cities overseas, such as Beijing and Manila.

訳：ちょっと信じられないだろうが、（　　　　　　　　　　　　　　　　　　）は、北京やマニ
　　ラのような（　　　　　　　　　　　　　　　　　）のだ。

● Report Completion

巻末 p. 128 にある **Report 14** の **Ⅲ** 〜 **Ⅴ** に答えましょう。

✏ Interview in Future Japan

🔊 43

大手自動車メーカーの広報担当者がインタビューを受けています。その音声を聴き、次の英文がインタビューの内容に合っていれば True に、合っていなければ False に ✓ を入れましょう

1. The spokesperson says the company is increasing the production of flying cars.　　□ True　□ False

2. The spokesperson says passengers should learn more about flying cars.　　□ True　□ False

3. The spokesperson says human drivers are not as intelligent as computers.　　□ True　□ False

Writing Composition

Analysis 本文中の〔　　〕内の表現を使って、次の日本語の意味を表す英文を完成させましょう。

1. その展示会で何十もの未来の乗り物を見ることできる。〔dozens of〕

We (　　　　　　) (　　　　　　　) (　　　　　　　) (　　　　　　)
(　　　　　　) (　　　　　　　) at the exhibition.

2. 空飛ぶ車が出す騒音は、あるとしてもすぐには解決されないだろう。〔if ever〕

The loud noise (　　　　　　) by (　　　　　　) (　　　　　　) will not be
solved soon, (　　　　　　) (　　　　　　).

3. 空飛ぶ車の開発は実現に近づいている。〔become closer to〕

The (　　　　　　) of (　　　　　　) (　　　　　　) is (　　　　　　)
(　　　　　　) (　　　　　　) reality.

4. ボタンを押してください、そうすればあなたのために残りはすべてそのコンピュータがします。〔the rest〕

Press the button, (　　　　　　) (　　　　　　) (　　　　　　) will do
(　　　　　　) (　　　　　　) (　　　　　　) (　　　　　　).

5. 空飛ぶ車の操作は陸上の乗り物ほど難しくはない。〔not as ... as〕

The operation of (　　　　　　) (　　　　　　) is (　　　　　　)
(　　　　　　) (　　　　　　) (　　　　　　) (　　　　　　)
(　　　　　　) surface vehicles.

44

First snowless year on Mt. Fuji

As Golden Week arrives, government officials in Shizuoka have declared the first snowless winter season on Mt. Fuji. This is the first time in recorded history that Fuji's <u>iconic</u> white top never appeared in winter. Ministry of the Environment official Seiji Okada said, "The year 2078 will <u>go down</u> in history. This is <u>highly</u> unusual, but not <u>unexpected</u>. Each year, we have <u>noted</u> that the <u>snow line</u> on Fuji is getting higher and higher. Recently, even in very snowy years, the snow line seldom goes below 3,000 meters." The Shizuoka <u>tourist board</u> announced that the newly-opened Fuji Ropeway, which runs right from the Fujinomiya Station 5 to the top of the crater <u>edge</u>, will open as usual this year on May 15. This is in line with the newly <u>revised</u> climbing season which now runs three months longer until October. 30.

 この記事のヘッドラインを日本語にしましょう。

Vocabulary Check

次の意味に該当するものを記事中の下線を引いた単語または語句から抜き出しましょう。ただし、動詞は原形で答えましょう。

1. 予想外の
   _____
2. …を注目する
   _____
3. …を改訂する
   _____
4. 降雪線
   _____
5. 端
   _____
6. おおいに
   _____
7. 象徴的な
   _____
8. 記録される
   _____
9. 珍しい
   _____
10. 観光局
    _____

Comprehension

空所に適語を記入して、記事の要旨を完成させましょう。

> ゴールデンウィークを控えて、静岡県は（　　　　　　　　　　　　　　　　　　
> 　　　　）ことを発表した。環境省のオカダセイジ氏は「これは（　　　　　　　）という
> ことではなく、富士山の降雪線は（　　　　　　　　　　　　　　　）、雪の多い年でも降雪
> 線が（　　　　　　　　　　　　　　　）は滅多にない」と述べた。なお、新たに開
> 業した（　　　　　　　　　　　　　）をつなぐ富士ロープウェイは、通年通りオー
> プンする。

Report Completion

巻末 p. 129 にある **Report 15** の Ⅰ と Ⅱ に答えましょう。

1   Mt. Fuji ranks high on almost any list of the world's most famous or beautiful mountains. Most often, images of Fuji show the symmetrical mountain with a white top and a blue sky background. Most people would agree that Fuji is most beautiful when it is covered in snow, which is usually from October to June.

2   However, there is no ①guarantee that Fuji's iconic snow cap will continue long into the future. Rising ②global temperatures mean that snow on Fuji will likely arrive later in the autumn and ③depart earlier in the spring. Current predictions are for a possible two-degree increase in the global temperature by the end of the century. Although this rise may seem small, it would have very serious effects. If it actually occurs, the lack of snow on Fuji will seem like a very minor problem compared to the challenges it will pose for Japan's farmers.

3   Mt. Kilimanjaro in Tanzania, whose glaciers will probably disappear in the next decade or two, provides ④a good comparison with Fuji. Although Kilimanjaro is much higher, it is also much closer to ⑤the equator, so the iconic snow and ice situation on the two mountains is similar. For both mountains, it is their ⑥snow-capped peaks that provide a special sense of beauty.

4   Fuji's almost perfect shape and snow cap will always be a big attraction for tourists. Over 300,000 people climb to the top most years. However, with a ropeway, these numbers could easily double or triple. As Japan becomes increasingly ⑦reliant on overseas tourists, building a ropeway to the top of Fuji would be ⑧a magnet to tourists around the world. However, in order to ⑨retain ⑩its worldwide fame, we have to hope that snow keeps falling on Fuji in the decades and centuries to come.

01
02
03
04
05
06
07
08
09
10
11
12
13
14
15
16
17
18
19
20
21
22

NOTES   symmetrical「左右対称の」 glacier「氷河」

Vocabulary Check

空所に適語を記入して、Analysis 本文中の下線を引いた単語や語句の意味を完成させましょう。

① (　　　　　　　　)　　　　　　⑥ 雪をいただいた（　　　　　　　）

② (　　　　　　　) 気温　　　　　⑦ 海外の観光客に（　　　　　　　）

③ (　　　　　　　　)　　　　　　⑧ 旅行者にとっての（　　　　　　）

④ よい（　　　　　　　）　　　　⑨ …を（　　　　　　）

⑤ (　　　　　　　　)　　　　　　⑩ その世界的な（　　　　　　）

96

Comprehension

Analysis 本文の各パラグラフにおいて、その主題文（1～2文）を抜き出しましょう。その後、各パラグラフに関する設問に答えましょう。

Paragraph❶

主題文： _____

📝 空所に適語を記入して、人々が最も美しいと思う富士山の姿を完成させましょう。

形が （　　　　　　　　　　）、頂上には （　　　　　　　）、背景には （　　　　　　　）。富士山は一般に
（　　　　　　　　　　） 10 月から 6 月が最も美しいとされる。

Paragraph❷

主題文： _____

📝 次の英文の内容が本文に合うように、空所に適する単語を記入しましょう。

1. The period when we can see snow on top of Fuji is likely to become (　　　　　)
because global temperatures are (　　　　　).

2. There are some (　　　　　) that the global temperature may be two degrees
(　　　　　) than now by the end of the 21st century.

3. The impact of global warming on (　　　　　) will be (　　　　　) serious than that
on Fuji.

Paragraph❸

主題文： _____

_____

📝 次の英文は、Mt. Kilimanjaro と Mt. Fuji のどちらに当てはまるでしょうか。該当するほうに
✓を入れましょう。なお、両方に当てはまる場合は Both に✓を入れましょう。

1. It is higher. ☐ Mt. Kilimanjaro ☐ Mt. Fuji ☐ Both
2. It is more distant to the equator. ☐ Mt. Kilimanjaro ☐ Mt. Fuji ☐ Both
3. It will be affected by global warming. ☐ Mt. Kilimanjaro ☐ Mt. Fuji ☐ Both
4. It is most beautiful with snow on top. ☐ Mt. Kilimanjaro ☐ Mt. Fuji ☐ Both

Paragraph❹

主題文：_____

_____

 次の質問に日本語で答えましょう。

1. over 300,000とは何の数値ですか。

_____

2. 1での数値は、どのようにすることで2倍、3倍になると予想されますか。

_____

3. 2で答えた状況が実現されるかもしれない理由を筆者はどのように述べていますか。

_____

_____

✓ Grammar Check　the が付かない形容詞の最上級

次の 2 つの文を比べてみましょう。

a. She is **the busiest** of us all.

b. She is **busiest** on Mondays.

a の文中にある形容詞の最上級 busiest には the が付いていますが、b の文中の busiest には付いていません。なぜでしょう？　a の文では他の人と比べていますが、b の文では自分の中で比べています。他の人や物と比べるとき、形容詞の最上級の後に名詞が省略されている（a の場合は person）ことが明らかな場合には the を付けます。それに対し、1 人の人［1 つの物］に関わる中での状況や性質として「いちばん…」というときには、形容詞の最上級に the を付けないのです。

 次の英文は Analysis 本文からの抜粋です。下線部に注意して、訳を完成させしましょう。

Most people would agree that Fuji is <u>most beautiful</u> when it is covered in snow, which is usually from October to June.

訳：富士山は（　　　　　　　　　　）とき、それはふつう（　　　　　　　　　　）なの
　　だが、そのときが（　　　　　　　　　　　　　　　　　　）同意するだろう。

● Report Completion

巻末 p. 130 にある **Report 15** の **Ⅲ** 〜 **Ⅴ** に答えましょう。

✏️ Interview in Future Japan 🔊 46

富士山の観光に訪れた外国人観光客が箱根でインタビューを受けています。その音声を聴き、次の英文がインタビューの内容に合っていれば True に、合っていなければ False に ✓ を入れましょう

1. The visitor came from Singapore to Hakone to see Mt. Fuji.   □ True □ False

2. The visitor is not completely pleased to see Mt. Fuji.   □ True □ False

3. The visitor will leave Hakone soon after the interview.   □ True □ False

Writing Composition

Analysis 本文中の [　　] 内の表現を使って、次の日本語の意味を表す英文を完成させましょう。

1. 冬には北海道の大雪山はすっぽり雪に覆われる。[be covered in]

Mt. Daisetsu in Hokkaido (　　　　　　) (　　　　　　) (　　　　　　)
(　　　　　　) (　　　　　　) (　　　　　　).

2. 今月末までに富士山に初雪が降るでしょう。[by the end of]

The (　　　　　　) (　　　　　　) will fall onto Mt. Fuji (　　　　　　)
(　　　　　　) (　　　　　　) (　　　　　　) (　　　　　　)
(　　　　　　).

3. 富士山は、その形が左右対称で、世界で最も美しい山の 1 つである。[whose]

Mt. Fuji, (　　　　　　) (　　　　　　) is symmetrical, is (　　　　　　)
(　　　　　　) (　　　　　　) (　　　　　　) (　　　　　　)
(　　　　　　) in the world.

4. 近ごろ、日本の小売業はますます海外の客に依存している。[reliant on]

These days, Japanese retail business (　　　　　　) increasingly
(　　　　　　) (　　　　　　) (　　　　　　) (　　　　　　).

5. 私は故郷に帰って自分の寝室の窓から富士山を見るときがいちばん幸せだ。
[the が付かない形容詞の最上級]

I (　　　　　　) (　　　　　　) when I (　　　　　　) (　　　　　　) my
hometown and see Mt. Fuji (　　　　　　) (　　　　　　) my bedroom
window.

Report 1

Student ID: _____

Name: _____

I 以下は、p. 10 の記事に描かれている日本の未来図とその背景をまとめたものです。空所に適語を記入して、各文を完成させましょう。

Prospective View

· _____ will no longer be produced

as of next month.

· As of January 1, 2041, all types of purchases will be _____

_____.

Background

· All cash will _____, so the public should _____

_____ to have it credited to their accounts

before December 31, 2040.

II その未来図が現実になる可能性は何パーセントだと考えますか。グラフに記入しましょう。

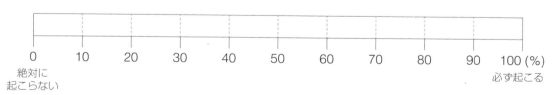

| 0 | 10 | 20 | 30 | 40 | 50 | 60 | 70 | 80 | 90 | 100 (%) |

絶対に　　　　　　　　　　　　　　　　　　　　　　　　　　　　　　必ず起こる
起こらない

Report 1

Ⅲ 次の意見に対する自分の考えを答えましょう。同意する場合は Agree に、同意しない場合は Disagree に ✓ を入れましょう。

1. E-commerce will increasingly become common. ☐ Agree ☐ Disagree

2. Japanese schoolchildren should learn about e-commerce as part of the school curriculum. ☐ Agree ☐ Disagree

3. In order to promote overseas visitors' purchases, Japan should spread cashless payments more rapidly. ☐ Agree ☐ Disagree

4. There is considerable concern about security with cashless payments. ☐ Agree ☐ Disagree

5. Paper notes and coins have a long history, so we should not abolish them completely. ☐ Agree ☐ Disagree

Ⅳ 記事で描かれている未来図が現実になる可能性は何パーセントかもう一度考え、グラフに記入しましょう。

```
0   10   20   30   40   50   60   70   80   90   100 (%)
絶対に                                          必ず起こる
起こらない
```

Ⅴ Ⅳのように考えたのはなぜですか。理由を書きましょう。

_____

_____

_____

Report 2

Student ID: _____

Name: _____

I 以下は、p. 16 の記事に描かれている日本の未来図とその背景をまとめたものです。空所に適語を記入して、各文を完成させましょう。

Prospective View

· Japanime, the popular Japanese theme park, received _____

than Disneyland.

· Japanime opened _____

in 2030, and now there are _____ outside of Japan.

Background

· Japanime is expanding around the world due to _____

_____.

II その未来図が現実になる可能性は何パーセントだと考えますか。グラフに記入しましょう。

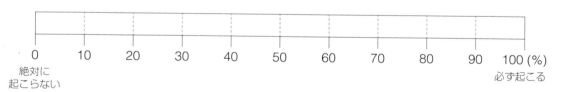

絶対に
起こらない 　　　　　　　　　　　　　　　　　　　　　　必ず起こる

Report **2**

Ⅲ 次の意見に対する自分の考えを答えましょう。同意する場合は Agree に、同意しない場合は Disagree に ✓ を入れましょう。

1. I feel it is Japanese culture that is attracting visitors from overseas.　☐ Agree　☐ Disagree

2. Japan should focus on anime to attract more overseas visitors.　☐ Agree　☐ Disagree

3. It is a good idea to let the world learn about Japan through anime.　☐ Agree　☐ Disagree

4. Japanese are not as good as Americans at building amusement parks.　☐ Agree　☐ Disagree

5. We may say that Pokémon has become a good rival of Mickey Mouse.　☐ Agree　☐ Disagree

Ⅳ 記事で描かれている未来図が現実になる可能性は何パーセントかもう一度考え、グラフに記入しましょう。

| 0 | 10 | 20 | 30 | 40 | 50 | 60 | 70 | 80 | 90 | 100 (%) |

絶対に
起こらない

必ず起こる

Ⅴ Ⅳのように考えたのはなぜですか。理由を書きましょう。

_____

_____

_____

Report **3**

Student ID: _____

Name: _____

I 以下は、p. 22 の記事に描かれている日本の未来図とその背景をまとめたものです。空所に適語を記入して、各文を完成させましょう。※（　）には単語または数字が 1 つずつ入ります。

Prospective View

· _____ has reached 30%.

· The level may reach (　　　　) % by (　　　　).

Background

· In Tokyo, buses, taxis and delivery vehicles are (　　　　).

· _____ are mostly

performed by computers.

· _____ are being affected by AI.

II その未来図が現実になる可能性は何パーセントだと考えますか。グラフに記入しましょう。

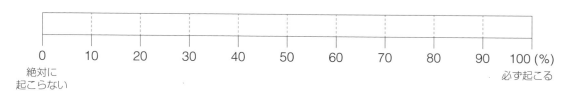

0　　10　　20　　30　　40　　50　　60　　70　　80　　90　　100 (%)

絶対に
起こらない　　　　　　　　　　　　　　　　　　　　　　　　　　必ず起こる

Report 3

Ⅲ 次の意見に対する自分の考えを答えましょう。同意する場合は Agree に、同意しない場合は Disagree に ✓ を入れましょう。

1. Buses or taxis will be driverless in the near future. Drivers will lose their jobs. ☐ Agree ☐ Disagree

2. More and more people will shop online. Salespeople will lose their jobs. ☐ Agree ☐ Disagree

3. Computers are able to create art, compose music and novels. Artists will lose their jobs. ☐ Agree ☐ Disagree

4. There is no need to worry. New jobs will be created when AI has replaced current occupations. ☐ Agree ☐ Disagree

5. There are some jobs that cannot be replaced by AI. ☐ Agree ☐ Disagree

Ⅳ 記事で描かれている未来図が現実になる可能性は何パーセントかもう一度考え、グラフに記入しましょう。

```
0    10    20    30    40    50    60    70    80    90    100 (%)
絶対に                                              必ず起こる
起こらない
```

Ⅴ Ⅳのように考えたのはなぜですか。理由を書きましょう。

_____

_____

_____

Report 4

Student ID: _____

Name: _____

I 以下は、p. 28 の記事に描かれている日本の未来図とその背景をまとめたものです。空所に適語を記入して、各文を完成させましょう。※（　）には単語が 1 つ入ります。

Prospective View

・McMoss, the fast food chain, has stopped making its hamburgers from

（　　　　　　）; they will be made of _____ from

now on.

Background

・McMoss found customers preferred _____.

・_____ of vegetarian burgers are getting

closer to meat burgers.

II その未来図が現実になる可能性は何パーセントだと考えますか。グラフに記入しましょう。

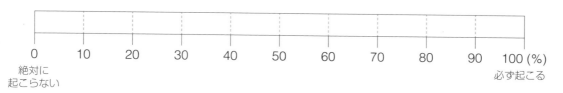

```
0    10    20    30    40    50    60    70    80    90   100 (%)
絶対に                                                      必ず起こる
起こらない
```

Report **4**

Ⅲ 次の意見に対する自分の考えを答えましょう。同意する場合は Agree に、同意しない場合は Disagree に ✓ を入れましょう。

1. These days, Japanese people are becoming more and more health-conscious. ☐ Agree ☐ Disagree

2. The government should not promote the import of meat from overseas. ☐ Agree ☐ Disagree

3. Now is the time for fast food restaurants to change their way of marketing. ☐ Agree ☐ Disagree

4. We should try not to kill animals for food as much as possible. ☐ Agree ☐ Disagree

5. In order to protect agriculture, the government should give more support to farmers. ☐ Agree ☐ Disagree

Ⅳ 記事で描かれている未来図が現実になる可能性は何パーセントかもう一度考え、グラフに記入しましょう。

| 0 | 10 | 20 | 30 | 40 | 50 | 60 | 70 | 80 | 90 | 100 (%) |

絶対に
起こらない

必ず起こる

Ⅴ Ⅳのように考えたのはなぜですか。理由を書きましょう。

_____

_____

_____

108

Report **5**

Student ID: _____

Name: _____

I 以下は、p. 34 の記事に描かれている日本の未来図とその背景をまとめたものです。空所に適語を記入して、各文を完成させましょう。

Prospective View

· The Shinkansen will _____ from

Tokyo to Kagoshima.

· _____ on April 25.

Background

· Using the Hyperloop, passengers will go _____ faster at

_____ to _____

where the present Shinkansen goes.

II その未来図が現実になる可能性は何パーセントだと考えますか。グラフに記入しましょう。

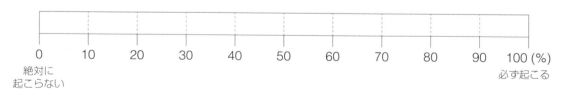

```
0    10    20    30    40    50    60    70    80    90   100 (%)
絶対に                                                    必ず起こる
起こらない
```

Report 5

Ⅲ　次の意見に対する自分の考えを答えましょう。同意する場合は Agree に、同意しない場合は Disagree に ✓ を入れましょう。

1. We have little land in Japan, so it is a good idea to have the Hyperloop instead of the Shinkansen.　☐ Agree　☐ Disagree

2. We should focus on flying vehicles as well as land vehicles.　☐ Agree　☐ Disagree

3. There will be many challenges in designing a perfectly comfortable Hyperloop.　☐ Agree　☐ Disagree

4. It is good to use driverless vehicles like the Hyperloop as public transportation.　☐ Agree　☐ Disagree

5. Environmental issues should come first in designing any vehicle.　☐ Agree　☐ Disagree

Ⅳ　記事で描かれている未来図が現実になる可能性は何パーセントかもう一度考え、グラフに記入しましょう。

```
┌───────────────────────────────────────────────┐
│                                               │
└───────────────────────────────────────────────┘
0    10   20   30   40   50   60   70   80   90  100 (%)
絶対に                                        必ず起こる
起こらない
```

Ⅴ　Ⅳのように考えたのはなぜですか。理由を書きましょう。

_____

_____

_____

Report **6**

Student ID: _____

Name: _____

I 以下は、p. 40 の記事に描かれている日本の未来図とその背景をまとめたものです。空所に適語を記入して、各文を完成させましょう。

Prospective View

· English will _____

_____ as of 2040.

· Computer coding _____ on the Center Test.

Background

· Now _____ are perfect.

· Now any written and spoken Japanese can be _____

_____ .

· When _____

are perfect, Chinese will also be removed from the test.

II その未来図が現実になる可能性は何パーセントだと考えますか。グラフに記入しましょう。

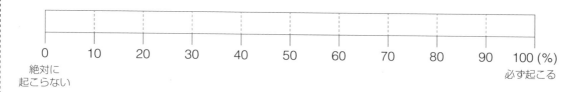

絶対に
起こらない

必ず起こる

Report 6

III 次の意見に対する自分の考えを答えましょう。同意する場合は Agree に、同意しない場合は Disagree に ✓ を入れましょう。

1. It won't be long before computer translation is perfect. ☐ Agree ☐ Disagree

2. With machine translators, people won't have to study foreign languages. ☐ Agree ☐ Disagree

3. Computer coding will be a more useful subject than foreign languages in the near future. ☐ Agree ☐ Disagree

4. People will lose interest in face-to-face communication in the future. ☐ Agree ☐ Disagree

5. With translation glasses and earphones, anybody will be able to travel anywhere with no problems. ☐ Agree ☐ Disagree

IV 記事で描かれている未来図が現実になる可能性は何パーセントかもう一度考え、グラフに記入しましょう。

| 0 | 10 | 20 | 30 | 40 | 50 | 60 | 70 | 80 | 90 | 100 (%) |

絶対に
起こらない

必ず起こる

V IVのように考えたのはなぜですか。理由を書きましょう。

_____

_____

_____

Report 7

Student ID: _____

Name: _____

I 以下は、p. 46 の記事に描かれている日本の未来図とその背景をまとめたものです。空所に適語を記入して、各文を完成させましょう。

Prospective View

· As of July 1, 2040, travelers _____

_____ for overseas travel.

· All travelers will _____ by using

biometrics.

Background

· In order to gather each traveler's information, smart cameras will _____

_____ .

· The new system _____ over the past years, so

tricking cameras will be impossible.

II その未来図が現実になる可能性は何パーセントだと考えますか。グラフに記入しましょう。

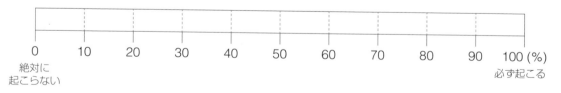

0 10 20 30 40 50 60 70 80 90 100 (%)

絶対に
起こらない

必ず起こる

Report **7**

Ⅲ 次の意見に対する自分の考えを答えましょう。同意する場合は Agree に、同意しない場合は Disagree に ✓ を入れましょう。

1. We should reduce the time to go through airport security. ☐ Agree ☐ Disagree

2. Facial recognition will be more and more effective in the future. ☐ Agree ☐ Disagree

3. Humans will sometimes be more effective than cameras. ☐ Agree ☐ Disagree

4. Time and convenience should come first in designing an airport. ☐ Agree ☐ Disagree

5. Airports all over the world will have similar biometric technology in the future. ☐ Agree ☐ Disagree

Ⅳ 記事で描かれている未来図が現実になる可能性は何パーセントかもう一度考え、グラフに記入しましょう。

| 0 | 10 | 20 | 30 | 40 | 50 | 60 | 70 | 80 | 90 | 100 (%) |

絶対に
起こらない

必ず起こる

Ⅴ Ⅳのように考えたのはなぜですか。理由を書きましょう。

_____

_____

_____

Report **8**

Student ID: _____

Name: _____

I 以下は、p. 52 の記事に描かれている日本の未来図とその背景をまとめたものです。空所に適語を記入して、各文を完成させましょう。

Prospective View

・Eleven Mart plans _____ to some

of its stores.

・They plan to _____

later next year or in 2042.

Background

・Customers prefer _____.

・Eleven Mart is looking for unique _____.

・In 2032, human staff _____ from convenience stores.

II その未来図が現実になる可能性は何パーセントだと考えますか。グラフに記入しましょう。

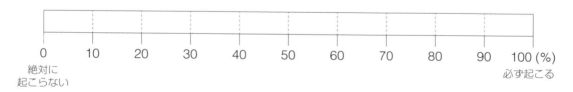

0　10　20　30　40　50　60　70　80　90　100 (%)
絶対に　　　　　　　　　　　　　　　　　　　　　　　必ず起こる
起こらない

115

Report 8

Ⅲ 次の意見に対する自分の考えを答えましょう。同意する場合は Agree に、同意しない場合は Disagree に✓を入れましょう。

1. Convenience stores should be as convenient as possible. ☐ Agree ☐ Disagree

2. What feels convenient is different from person to person, so there should be various options. ☐ Agree ☐ Disagree

3. For security, automated purchases without human staff is best only for stores that are open late at night. ☐ Agree ☐ Disagree

4. Replacing machines with humans goes against the trend, so the Eleven Mart's plan will be unsuccessful. ☐ Agree ☐ Disagree

5. Humanoids will be able to serve customers who want interaction with human staff. ☐ Agree ☐ Disagree

Ⅳ 記事で描かれている未来図が現実になる可能性は何パーセントかもう一度考え、グラフに記入しましょう。

```
  ┌──┬──┬──┬──┬──┬──┬──┬──┬──┬──┐
  0    10   20   30   40   50   60   70   80   90  100 (%)
絶対に                                              必ず起こる
起こらない
```

Ⅴ Ⅳのように考えたのはなぜですか。理由を書きましょう。

_____

_____

_____

Report 9

Student ID: _____

Name: _____

I 以下は、p. 58 の記事に描かれている日本の未来図とその背景をまとめたものです。空所に適語を記入して、各文を完成させましょう。※（　）には単語が 1 つ入ります。

Prospective View

· Japanese astronauts were the first _____

_____.

· The JMT won the prize in _____ by defeating

_____.

Background

· In 2032, _____

announced the competition.

· The Japanese astronauts plan to spend _____ conducting

(_____) there.

· JMT team will _____ in 2042.

II その未来図が現実になる可能性は何パーセントだと考えますか。グラフに記入しましょう。

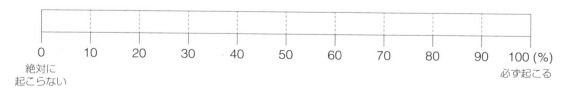

```
  0    10   20   30   40   50   60   70   80   90  100 (%)
絶対に                                          必ず起こる
起こらない
```

Report 9

Ⅲ 次の意見に対する自分の考えを答えましょう。同意する場合は Agree に、同意しない場合は Disagree に ✓ を入れましょう。

1. It is worthwhile to spend money on space technology for our future. ☐ Agree ☐ Disagree

2. Psychological problems would be much bigger than technical ones in successfully traveling to Mars. ☐ Agree ☐ Disagree

3. To land on Mars would be meaningless to humans because the planet is too difficult to live on. ☐ Agree ☐ Disagree

4. We should not compete in space development. We should solve problems on Earth first. ☐ Agree ☐ Disagree

5. It is natural for humans to have the desire to explore the unknown world. ☐ Agree ☐ Disagree

Ⅳ 記事で描かれている未来図が現実になる可能性は何パーセントかもう一度考え、グラフに記入しましょう。

```
|----|----|----|----|----|----|----|----|----|----|
0    10   20   30   40   50   60   70   80   90  100 (%)
絶対に                                              必ず起こる
起こらない
```

Ⅴ Ⅳのように考えたのはなぜですか。理由を書きましょう。

_____

_____

_____

Report **10**

Student ID: _____

Name: _____

I 以下は、p. 64 の記事に描かれている日本の未来図とその背景をまとめたものです。空所に適語を記入して、各文を完成させましょう。※ （ ）には数字が入ります。

Prospective View

・Japan became _____ of NPTO.

・With Japan, NPTO is _____

_____ in the world.

Background

・In 2035, China and Korea _____,

and discussions ended with a breakthrough last month.

・_____ will be the next big challenge,

and it will be achieved by (   ).

II その未来図が現実になる可能性は何パーセントだと考えますか。グラフに記入しましょう。

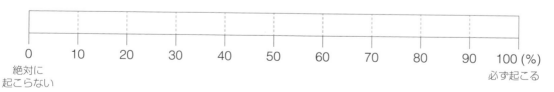

0   10   20   30   40   50   60   70   80   90   100 (%)

絶対に
起こらない   必ず起こる

Report **10**

Ⅲ 次の意見に対する自分の考えを答えましょう。同意する場合は Agree に、同意しない場合は Disagree に ✓ を入れましょう。

1. Asian countries should form a powerful block to compete with other blocks in the world. ☐ Agree ☐ Disagree

2. Japan should lead the other Asian countries in terms of economic development. ☐ Agree ☐ Disagree

3. To form a common currency among Asian neighbors has more advantages than disadvantages. ☐ Agree ☐ Disagree

4. We should learn some lessons from the European Union. ☐ Agree ☐ Disagree

5. If there is an economic advantage, we should sometimes give up our cultural uniqueness. ☐ Agree ☐ Disagree

Ⅳ 記事で描かれている未来図が現実になる可能性は何パーセントかもう一度考え、グラフに記入しましょう。

```
    0   10   20   30   40   50   60   70   80   90  100 (%)
  絶対に                                              必ず起こる
  起こらない
```

Ⅴ Ⅳのように考えたのはなぜですか。理由を書きましょう。

_____

_____

_____

Report **11**

Student ID: _____

Name: _____

I 以下は、p. 70 の記事に描かれている日本の未来図とその背景をまとめたものです。空所に適語を記入して、各文を完成させましょう。

Prospective View

· The government's statistics reveal that Japan's population in 2040 _____

_____.

· The population _____ by 2060.

Background

· The new average lifespan for women _____ and

for men _____.

· _____ have helped people live longer.

II その未来図が現実になる可能性は何パーセントだと考えますか。グラフに記入しましょう。

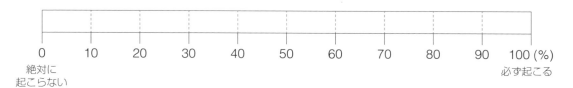

0　10　20　30　40　50　60　70　80　90　100 (%)

絶対に
起こらない   必ず起こる

Report **11**

Ⅲ 次の意見に対する自分の考えを答えましょう。同意する場合は Agree に、同意しない場合は Disagree に ✓ を入れましょう。

1. It is not such a big problem if the population decreases. ☐ Agree ☐ Disagree

2. The government should support Japanese researchers to bring about more medical advances. ☐ Agree ☐ Disagree

3. Japanese society is not helpful enough for women who want to bear children. ☐ Agree ☐ Disagree

4. Japan will accept more immigrants in the future. ☐ Agree ☐ Disagree

5. The aging population is a more serious problem than the decrease in population. ☐ Agree ☐ Disagree

Ⅳ 記事で描かれている未来図が現実になる可能性は何パーセントかもう一度考え、グラフに記入しましょう。

0	10	20	30	40	50	60	70	80	90	100 (%)

絶対に
起こらない　　　　　　　　　　　　　　　　　　　　　　　　　　　必ず起こる

Ⅴ Ⅳのように考えたのはなぜですか。理由を書きましょう。

_____

_____

_____

Report **12**

Student ID: _____

Name: _____

I 以下は、p. 76 の記事に描かれている日本の未来図とその背景をまとめたものです。空所に適語を記入して、各文を完成させましょう。

Prospective View

· Japan's two biggest beer companies announced _____

_____ .

Background

· _____ was the lowest on record last year.

· The amount of _____ people drink is decreasing,

and _____ have kept going down.

· The _____ prefers non-alcohol drinks, and _____

_____ are drinking less or dying off.

II その未来図が現実になる可能性は何パーセントだと考えますか。グラフに記入しましょう。

```
|----|----|----|----|----|----|----|----|----|----|
0    10   20   30   40   50   60   70   80   90   100 (%)
絶対に                                              必ず起こる
起こらない
```

Report **12**

Ⅲ 次の意見に対する自分の考えを答えましょう。同意する場合は Agree に、同意しない場合は Disagree に✓を入れましょう。

1. It has become old-fashioned to drink beer or sake with bosses after work.　☐ Agree　☐ Disagree

2. One's family should have priority over work for both men and women.　☐ Agree　☐ Disagree

3. Japanese society has been slow to change with regard to gender roles.　☐ Agree　☐ Disagree

4. Young Japanese should learn more about the risks of alcohol.　☐ Agree　☐ Disagree

5. It is foolish to spend money on alcohol.　☐ Agree　☐ Disagree

Ⅳ 記事で描かれている未来図が現実になる可能性は何パーセントかもう一度考え、グラフに記入しましょう。

```
 |____|____|____|____|____|____|____|____|____|____|
 0    10   20   30   40   50   60   70   80   90  100 (%)
絶対に                                           必ず起こる
起こらない
```

Ⅴ Ⅳのように考えたのはなぜですか。理由を書きましょう。

_____

_____

_____

Report **13**

Student ID: _____

Name: _____

I 以下は、p. 82 の記事に描かれている日本の未来図とその背景をまとめたものです。空所に適語を記入して、各文を完成させましょう。

Prospective View

・The school year will _____.

・English will be used as _____

_____.

・_____

will be held in virtual mode.

Background

・Japanese students should be _____

_____.

II その未来図が現実になる可能性は何パーセントだと考えますか。グラフに記入しましょう。

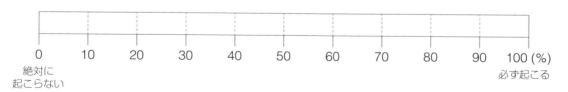

0   10   20   30   40   50   60   70   80   90   100 (%)

絶対に
起こらない   必ず起こる

Report **13**

Ⅲ 次の意見に対する自分の考えを答えましょう。同意する場合は Agree に、同意しない場合は Disagree に ✔ を入れましょう。

1. For international students, Japanese universities should provide instruction in English. ☐ Agree ☐ Disagree

2. Japanese universities should start in September as in most of the world. ☐ Agree ☐ Disagree

3. MOOCs will be more useful than traditional face-to-face courses. ☐ Agree ☐ Disagree

4. Students will submit their assignments in multimedia format instead of writing essays. ☐ Agree ☐ Disagree

5. Students will not have to study grammar or vocabulary as machines will do it all for them. ☐ Agree ☐ Disagree

Ⅳ 記事で描かれている未来図が現実になる可能性は何パーセントかもう一度考え、グラフに記入しましょう。

| 0 | 10 | 20 | 30 | 40 | 50 | 60 | 70 | 80 | 90 | 100 (%) |

絶対に
起こらない

必ず起こる

Ⅴ Ⅳのように考えたのはなぜですか。理由を書きましょう。

_____

_____

_____

Report **14**

Student ID: _____

Name: _____

I 以下は、p. 88 の記事に描かれている日本の未来図とその背景をまとめたものです。空所に適語を記入して、各文を完成させましょう。

Prospective View

· Two flying cars _____,

and two people were killed.

· Some clues suggest that _____

_____.

Background

· It was the first fatal accident since _____

_____ in 2049.

· It appears that many of the safety mechanisms _____.

II その未来図が現実になる可能性は何パーセントだと考えますか。グラフに記入しましょう。

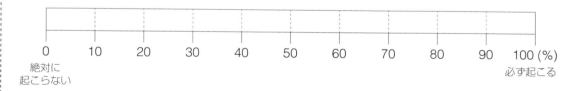

0 10 20 30 40 50 60 70 80 90 100 (%)

絶対に
起こらない

必ず起こる

Report **14**

Ⅲ 次の意見に対する自分の考えを答えましょう。同意する場合は Agree に、同意しない場合は Disagree に ✓ を入れましょう。

1. Rules for flying cars will be complicated, so it will take considerable time to prepare laws. ☐ Agree ☐ Disagree

2. Licenses will be unnecessary to operate flying cars. ☐ Agree ☐ Disagree

3. Accidents will happen with any vehicle. Flying cars are no exception. ☐ Agree ☐ Disagree

4. Artificial intelligence is more reliable than human intelligence. ☐ Agree ☐ Disagree

5. In the beginning, the price of flying cars will be high, so it will take time for them to be available for mass private use. ☐ Agree ☐ Disagree

Ⅳ 記事で描かれている未来図が現実になる可能性は何パーセントかもう一度考え、グラフに記入しましょう。

```
┌─────┬─────┬─────┬─────┬─────┬─────┬─────┬─────┬─────┬─────┐
0    10    20    30    40    50    60    70    80    90    100 (%)
```
絶対に
起こらない　　　　　　　　　　　　　　　　　　　　　　　　　　　　必ず起こる

Ⅴ Ⅳのように考えたのはなぜですか。理由を書きましょう。

_____

_____

_____

Report **15**

Student ID: _____

Name: _____

I 以下は、p. 94 の記事に描かれている日本の未来図とその背景をまとめたものです。空所に適語を記入して、各文を完成させましょう。

Prospective View

· Mt Fuji had the first _____, and its white top _____

_____.

Background

· The snow line on Fuji has been getting _____,

and it seldom _____.

· The climbing season was revised from _____ until _____

_____.

II その未来図が現実になる可能性は何パーセントだと考えますか。グラフに記入しましょう。

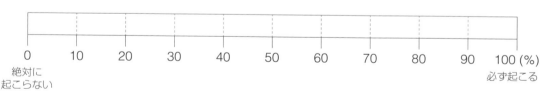

0　　10　　20　　30　　40　　50　　60　　70　　80　　90　　100 (%)

絶対に
起こらない

必ず起こる

Report **15**

Ⅲ 次の意見に対する自分の考えを答えましょう。同意する場合は Agree に、同意しない場合は Disagree に ✓ を入れましょう。

1. Mt. Fuji's snowcap has become iconic. ☐ Agree ☐ Disagree

2. It is a good idea to install a ropeway to the crater edge to attract more visitors. ☐ Agree ☐ Disagree

3. It is inevitable that climate change will have an effect on nature. We should accept that. ☐ Agree ☐ Disagree

4. Technology will find a solution to keep snow falling on Mt. Fuji. ☐ Agree ☐ Disagree

5. Aside from Mt. Fuji, we should consider the influence of global warming on farming. ☐ Agree ☐ Disagree

Ⅳ 記事で描かれている未来図が現実になる可能性は何パーセントかもう一度考え、グラフに記入しましょう。

| 0 | 10 | 20 | 30 | 40 | 50 | 60 | 70 | 80 | 90 | 100 (%) |

絶対に
起こらない

必ず起こる

Ⅴ Ⅳのように考えたのはなぜですか。理由を書きましょう。

_____

_____

_____

クラス用音声 CD 有り（別売）

Future Times — News Reports from Japan's Next Generation
日本社会の未来予想図を読んで考える

2020 年 1 月 20 日　初版発行
2023 年 2 月 10 日　第 4 刷

著　　者　Paul Stapleton、上村淳子
発 行 者　松村達生
発 行 所　センゲージ ラーニング株式会社

〒 102-0073　東京都千代田区九段北 1-11-11　第 2 フナトビル 5 階
電話　03-3511-4392
FAX　03-3511-4391
e-mail: eltjapan@cengage.com
copyright © 2020 センゲージ ラーニング株式会社

装　　丁　森村直美
組　　版　（有）トライアングル
印刷・製本　錦明印刷株式会社

ISBN 978-4-86312-367-0